The Covering

God's Plan to Protect You from Evil

Hank Hanegraaff

Thomas Nelson
Since 1798

To Grace Fabian,
who wears the helmet of salvation as a covering;
and to Grace Hanegraaff,
who exchanged her helmet for a crown.

THE COVERING
by Hank Hanegraaff

ISBN 978-0-8499-2917-5 (trade paper)

Printed in the United States of America
HB 03.03.2023

CONTENTS

ACKNOWLEDGMENTS

First, a word of thanks to the board, staff, and friends of the Christian Research Institute for their prayers. They were not just my covering; they were my comfort. Furthermore, I'd like to thank Stephen Ross for his insights, Elliot Miller for his feedback, Gretchen Passantino and Lee Strobel for their encouragement and suggestions, and Mark Sweeney and the entire W Publishing team for their support and editing expertise. Finally, my love and gratitude to Kathy and our kids—Michelle, Katie, David, John Mark, Hank Jr., Christina, Paul Stephen, Faith, and baby Grace, who preceeded us to heaven. Above all, I am supremely grateful for my heavenly Father, who wears "righteousness as his breastplate" (Isaiah 59:17).

INTRODUCTION

One of the inescapable realities of the Christian worldview is that "our struggle is not against flesh and blood, but against the rulers, against the authorities, against the powers of this dark world and against the spiritual forces of evil in the heavenly realms" (Ephesians 6:12). Put another way, you and I are engaged in a war against an invisible enemy. And as with our war on terrorism, the West is suddenly preoccupied with finding strategies for winning this invisible war.

Amazon.com now lists more than five hundred titles on spiritual warfare, and the Internet search engine Google has identified fifty thousand-plus references to Christian spiritual warfare. As Christian scholar Dr. Clinton Arnold has well said, "At no time in the history of the church has more been written about the topic of spiritual warfare than in the past decade. It appears that more Christians are thinking about spiritual warfare now than they have for at least a couple of centuries."[1]

Ironically, it wasn't all that long ago that Satan seemed all but dead and buried—the casualty of a modernist mind-set bent on rationalizing the supernatural out of existence. But as modernism yielded to the spirituality of postmodernism, Satan reappeared with a vengeance. The expression of Satan that emerged, however, was no longer based on a Christian worldview. Instead, a cultural caricature driven by the entertainment industry sprang into existence.

One of the defining moments in Satan's reemergence came in 1973, when William Peter Blatty's *The Exorcist* hit the silver screen. America watched breathlessly as Regan became the poster child for demonization. Mysterious satanic markings appeared on the body of actress Linda Blair. And that was only the beginning. Hollywood titillated the masses with sexually perverse language and sensationally produced levitation episodes.

AMERICA'S FASCINATION WITH THE DEMONIC

A number of nineteenth and twentieth-century ideas combined to prepare our culture for its current fascination with the demonic. In the nineteenth century, the rise of spiritualism——the belief in the existence of intercommunication with the dead——prepared the way for such sophisticated movie blockbusters as The Sixth Sense *or television's* The X-Files.[2]

The psychoanalysis of Freud bridged the nineteenth and twentieth centuries with the now commonly accepted belief that one's current maladies (physical, mental, and emotional) could be blamed on one's past traumatic experiences. The presence of the malady, Freud and his successors argued, "proved" the presence of the past traumas, without any empirical evidence.[3]

The last half of the twentieth century laid a foundation of credulity and superstition held together by pseudoscience, public spectacle, and personal experience. The decadence of the 1960s was epitomized in the newspaper pictures of Anton Szandor Lavey's celebration of the "black mass" on the altar of a naked woman. Lavey formed the church of Satan in 1965 and published the Satanic Bible in 1968 in a bid for public adoration exemplified by Hollywood's ode to Satanism, 1968's movie Rosemary's Baby.[4]

The 1980s and 1990s gave way to the great Satanism scare, the twentieth century's counterpart to colonial America's Salem witch trials. The great Satanism scare accelerated with the rumors of a vast, international, multigenerational, nearly undetectable satanic conspiracy described in 1983's Michelle Remembers. *It came to full force in the Christianized "satanic panic" of* Satan's Underground *and* The Satan Seller. *Unsubstantiated, sensational personal testimonies fostered an unprecedented period of criminal prosecution, psychiatric institutionalization, and family disintegration.*[5]

Millions of modernists who had attempted to rationalize supernatural evil out of existence suddenly began embracing Flip Wilson theology with a vengeance. Seemingly overnight the new mantra of the materialistic masses became "The devil made me do it." People from across the sociological spectrum were certain they housed demons, and demand for deliverance skyrocketed.

Tragically, the fascination with demons in the culture

at large has now led to a robust deliverance movement within evangelicalism. As anthropologist Michael Cuneo explains, one would be hard-pressed to come up with a better scheme. "Whatever one's personal problem—depression, anxiety, substance addiction, or even a runaway sexual appetite—there are exorcism ministries available today that will happily claim expertise for dealing with it. With the significant bonus, moreover, that one is not, for the most part, held personally responsible for the problem. Indwelling demons are mainly to blame, and getting rid of them is the key to moral and psychological redemption."[6]

In *American Exorcism,* Cuneo traces the spread of deliverance mania from popular culture to Christianity—from *The Exorcist* to evangelical exorcism ministries.[7] He notes that the demand for deliverance spurred by *The Exorcist* may well have died out were it not for the 1976 release of *Hostage to the Devil* by controversial Jesuit priest Malachi Martin. Despite demonstrating "a remarkable talent for fabrication and embellishment—for converting, by literary sleight-of-hand, half-truths and innuendo into immutable facts of history,"[8] Martin succeeded in fanning the exorcism flame into a veritable inferno.

That same year Ed and Lorraine Warren, billed as "the World's Most Famous Demonologists," hit prime time as a result of what would come to be known as the *Amityville Horror.* The Warrens pronounced a house in Amityville, Long Island—the scene of multiple murders—cursed and conducted a televised séance on the site.[9] In the predictable media frenzy that ensued, the Warrens portrayed Amityville as a microcosm of demonic activity in America.[10]

In books and movies that followed *(Ghost Hunters, The Haunted,* et al), the Warrens told lurid tales of mysterious bathroom markings and demonic beings that could scratch and claw their victims. They even recast the incubi and succubi of medieval mythology in contemporary prose. According to the Warrens, these male and female sexual demons frequented the homes of middle-class Americans, pillaging women and pleasuring men.[11]

As people struggled to come to grips with the demonic in the decade following the debut of *The Exorcist,* best-selling author and psychotherapist M. Scott Peck provided the deliverance craze with some much-needed legitimacy.[12] In the 1983 release of *People of the Lie,* the Harvard/Columbia-trained psychiatrist argued that exorcism was not only heroic, but it provided the only recourse for many of his troubled patients.[13]

While confiding that his views on exorcism had been initiated by *The Exorcist* and informed by *Hostage to the Devil,*[14] Peck provided the deliverance industry the air of respectability it desperately needed.[15] Says Cuneo, "In the years that followed the publication of *People of the Lie,* America's backseat romance with exorcism gradually gave way to a full-fledged cultural fascination with Satanism."[16]

This fascination with demons in the culture at large would inexorably lead to a robust spiritual warfare movement within evangelicalism. Having lost the ability to think biblically, postmodern believers were quickly transformed from cultural change agents and initiators into cultural conformists and imitators. Pop culture beckoned, and postmodern Christians took the bait. As a result, the discipleship model of spiritual warfare once championed by

Puritans in premodern America has given way to a deliverance motif. Put another way, the Puritan passion for exercising spiritual disciplines in order to become like Christ has given way to the quick fix of exorcising demons.

Leading the deliverance craze are men like Bob Larson, who is convinced that demons can trigger hundreds of independent fire alarms simultaneously,[17] materialize dangerous weapons out of thin air,[18] tamper with car brakes,[19] and cause earthquakes registering 5.0 on the Richter scale.[20] Larson's foray into the field of live public exorcisms has resulted in dramatic encounters with a wide assortment of foul spirits, including what he describes as "sexual demons." In one of his books, Larson recounts the story of a counselee who needed an abortion after being "assaulted by a sexual demon of incubus." Says Larson, "We countered this demonic impregnation with prayer and commanded that Satan's supernatural offspring be aborted."[21]

Like Larson, Dr. Neil Anderson believes in sexual demons. In his view, interaction between humans and sexual demons is "an experience common enough to be included in the first of his seven 'steps to freedom' as a possible past sin to be renounced."[22] Anderson is also convinced that satanic ritual abuse and multiple personality disorder are common problems caused by a vast satanic conspiracy. Says Anderson, "There are breeders out there. Now we've encountered people who are doctors and lawyers and pastors that are Satanists, disguising themselves as ministers of righteousness."[23] Anderson notes that he has "counseled enough victims of Satanism to know that there are breeders (producing children expressly for sacrifice or for development into leaders) and infiltrators committed to infiltrating and disrupting Christian ministry."[24]

In his bestseller *The Bondage Breaker,* Anderson describes how the forces of darkness targeted him personally for purposing to expose Satan's strategies: "When I stepped out of the shower I found several strange symbols traced on the fogged-up mirror. . . . I went down to eat breakfast alone, and as I was sitting in the kitchen, suddenly I felt a slight pain on my hand that made me flinch. I looked down to see what appeared to be two little bite-marks on my hand. 'Is that your best shot?' I said to the powers of darkness attacking me. 'Do you think symbols on the mirror and a little bite are going to keep me from giving my message in chapel today? Get out of here.'"[25]

He warns that "Satanists meet from 12:00 to 3:00 A.M., and part of their ritual is to summon and send demons. Three in the morning is the prime time for demon activity, and if you have awakened at that time it may be that you have been targeted. I have been targeted by demons numerous times."[26] Anderson warns that adopted children are especially vulnerable to demonic strongholds,[27] that the monsters children see at night in their rooms are demons that must be rebuked in the name of Jesus,[28] and that evil spirits are prone to attach themselves to physical objects.[29]

Anderson and Larson no doubt disagree on various aspects of spiritual warfare, but they share the belief that Christians are primary targets for demonization. According to Anderson, an astounding 85 percent of the evangelical Christian community is ensnared in some level of satanic bondage.[30] And Larson goes so far as to argue that believers have no business trying "to cast a demon out of somebody who isn't a Christian."[31]

This belief is by no means unique. During the past thirty years, a veritable who's who in Christianity have added support to the notion that Christians can be demonized and that deliverance is the cure.[32] Most confess that they were once unconvinced, but pastoral experience forced them to rethink their theological paradigms. Don Basham, author of the well-circulated *Deliver Us from Evil,* is a classic case in point.

Shortly after immersing himself in the deliverance ministry, Basham was struck by the realization that all of his exorcisms involved born-again believers who had been baptized in the Holy Spirit. Aware that his experience was in conflict with the Bible and Pentecostal theology, Basham sought counsel from a former Cambridge philosophy professor named Derek Prince, who had become an experienced deliverance minister.[33]

Prince pointed out that 95 percent of the people who experienced genuine deliverance were sincere believers. He went on to note that he had been personally exorcized of the demon of anger. As Prince explained, "It was as if some heaviness, some weight, was dislodged from inside my chest cavity and passed out through my mouth. I distinctly felt *something* leave."[34] Prince conceded that there was no direct biblical evidence for a Christian falling prey to demonization. However, in his view, the experiential evidence was overwhelming. Thus, his change of heart was prompted by subjective experience rather than scriptural evidence.[35]

And that is precisely the point. Subjective experiences are notoriously unreliable. Thus, they must always be tested in light of the objective truths of Scripture.[36] In the pages that follow I will demonstrate that the key to victory in the invisible war is not found in deliverance, but in discipleship. While we must give the devil his due, we dare not overestimate his power and province. Sexual spirits, devils that bite, and faddish formulas for freedom are but the fleeting fancy of pop culture and pagan superstition.

The covering described in Scripture as the full armor of God, however, is an impenetrable barrier against which the fiery darts of the evil one are impotent. When we are clothed in the covering, we are invincible. When we are not, we are but pawns in the devil's malevolent schemes.

My passion for writing *The Covering* was born out of my previous book *The Prayer of Jesus*. In the last petition of this model prayer, Jesus taught his disciples to pray, "Lead us not into temptation, but deliver us from the evil one" (Matthew 6:13). When you do, you should be immediately reminded to "put on the full armor of God so that you can take your stand against the devil's schemes" (Ephesians 6:11). That, of course, means that you are not only intimately acquainted with each piece of the armor described by Paul in Ephesians 6, but you understand what each piece represents.

When I finished writing *The Prayer of Jesus,* I told my wife, Kathy, that if I had written it for no one but myself, it would have been well worth the effort. It has absolutely revolutionized my personal prayer life. My only regret was that size and space did not permit me to flesh out the full armor of God. Thus, I am thrilled to have the opportunity to do so in this sequel.

ONE

The Devil Made Me Do It

*Finally, be strong in the Lord and in his mighty power.
Put on the full armor of God so that you can take your stand
against the devil's schemes. (Ephesians 6:10–11)*

It was a moment I will never forget. I can still remember exactly where I was and what I was doing when I first heard Dr. Clinton Arnold tell the story. He was engaged in a debate with Elliott Miller, editor-in-chief of the *Christian Research Journal,* on the subject of "The Christian and Demonic Influence." As Arnold neared the end of the opening presentation, he told the story of Wycliffe Bible translator Edmund Fabian, who was brutally murdered in Papua New Guinea.[1]

As prologue, Arnold communicated his conviction that "there's a great danger, and sometimes even a life-and-death danger" in thinking that a Christian cannot be inhabited by a demon. He went on to note that the murder of Edmund Fabian prompted Wycliffe "to rethink their position on the relationship of the demonic to believers."

According to Arnold, Edmund Fabian made the fatal mistake of assuming that Rin, his Christian translation consultant, could not possibly be demon-possessed. Despite Rin's claims that a powerful voice in his head kept telling him to pick up a hatchet and strike Edmund on the head, Edmund told Rin to "quit worrying that it might be an evil spirit—demons can't possess Christians." In time Rin yielded to the demon's command, picked up a hatchet, and brutally murdered Edmund Fabian.

While I had heard or read hundreds of stories regarding so-called demonized Christians over the years, the story of Edmund Fabian's death gripped me like no other. Perhaps it was because Arnold is arguably the most credible Christian leader who defends the notion that Christians can be demonized. Or perhaps it was the import of the words "there is a great danger, and sometimes even a life-and-death danger."

If ever there was an example of ideas having consequences, this was it! For all intents and purposes, Edmund had signed his own death certificate by stubbornly refusing to believe that Christians could be inhabited by demons. Worse yet, the gory image of Edmund's death forced me to consider the possibility that I might also be guilty of lulling Christians into a false sense of security. If Edmund's murder had caused a world-class missions organization like Wycliffe to rethink its position on the demonization of believers, maybe I should reconsider my beliefs as well.

BACK TO THE BIBLE

Edmund Fabian's death caused me to experience a genuine psychological paradox. On the one hand, I was certain that Scripture precluded the possibility of Christian demonization. On the other, I had no doubt that Arnold's account of Edmund's death at the hands of a demon-possessed Christian was carefully researched and credible. In the end it was this emotional tension that drove me to take a closer look at both Scripture and the story.

As I dove back into the Bible, I was comforted to discover that Christ himself precludes the possibility that a Christian could be inhabited by demons. Using the illustration of a house, Jesus asks, "How can anyone enter a strong man's house and carry off his possessions unless he first ties up the strong man?" (Matthew 12:29). In the case of a demon-possessed person, the strong man is obviously the devil. In a Spirit-indwelt believer, however, the strong man is God. The force of Christ's argument leads inexorably to the conclusion that, in order for demons to possess believers, they would first have to bind the one who occupies them—namely God himself!

Jesus provides a corollary argument by pointing out, "When an evil spirit comes out of a man, it goes through arid places seeking rest and does not find it. Then it says, 'I will return to the house I left.' When it arrives, it finds the house *unoccupied,* swept clean and put in order. Then it goes and takes with it seven other spirits more wicked than itself, and they go in and live there. And the final condition of that man is worse than the first" (Matthew 12:43–45; emphasis added). The point here is pristine and precise: If we are unoccupied by the Holy Spirit, we subject ourselves to the possibility of being inhabited by demons. If, on the other hand, our house is Christ's home, the devil finds no place in us.

Furthermore, I discovered an equally airtight argument against Christian demonization in the Gospel of John. The Jews were once again accusing Jesus of being demon-possessed. Rather than circumvent their accusations, Jesus reaches out to his accusers with reason. The essence of his argument is, "I am not possessed by a demon" because "I honor my Father" (John 8:49). Once again the point is impossible to miss: Being demon-possessed and honoring God are mutually exclusive categories![2]

Finally, as I poured through the pages of Scripture, not a single credible example of a demonized believer emerged. Instead, the con-sistent teaching of Scripture is that Christians cannot be con-trolled against their wills through demonic inhabitation.

> *The consistent teaching of Scripture is that Christians cannot be controlled against their wills through demonic inhabitation.*

The principle is foolproof. If you are a follower of Christ, the King himself indwells you (see John 14:23; Romans 8:9–17). And you can rest assured that "the

one who is in you is greater than the one who is in the world"
(1 John 4:4).

Searching the Scriptures more than satisfied me intel-
lectually. If Christ communicates that honoring God and
being demon-possessed are mutually exclusive categories,
and if the Bible does not contain a single credible example
of a demonized Christian, the matter was settled in my
head. In my heart, however, I still struggled with the
emotional impact of Edmund Fabian's brutal murder.

CAN A BELIEVER BE DEMONIZED?

*It is telling that those who persist in overestimating the power
and province of Satan have had to resort to using the story of
the crippled woman chronicled in Luke 13 as "a fairly clear
case of a believer who has been demonized."[3]*

*Their argument is typically forwarded as follows: The
woman Jesus encountered "had been crippled by a spirit for
eighteen years"; she was in the synagogue; and she was referred
to as "a daughter of Abraham." Consequently, she must have been
a demonized believer. This, however, is far from true. To begin*

19

with, this narrative in Luke lacks all the common features of an exorcism account. Jesus addresses the woman rather than addressing a demon; Satan does not speak through the crippled woman, but she remains silent until Jesus heals her; and not only Luke, but the synagogue ruler refers to what happened as a healing, rather than an exorcism.

Even if we grant that this was an exorcism, the fact that Jesus encountered the crippled woman in the synagogue does not make her a Christian. Christ encountered all kinds of people in the synagogue who were not believers. In fact, he referred to the rabbis who taught the law in the synagogue as "hypocrites," "blind guides," "a brood of vipers," and "whitewashed tombs, which look beautiful on the outside but on the inside are full of dead men's bones and everything unclean"(Matthew 23:13, 16, 27, 33). Moreover, the fact that Jesus referred to the crippled woman as "a daughter of Abraham" does not of necessity make her a demon-possessed Christian. Jesus referred to Zacchaeus as "a son of Abraham," despite the fact that he was clearly not a believer at the time (Luke 19:9). In reality, the phrase "daughter of Abraham" implies nothing more than physical descent. As Scripture explicitly teaches, not all who are descended from Abraham have the faith of Abraham (see Romans 9:7–8; cf. Matthew 3:9).

THE STORY OF GRACE

I was spellbound as I watched Grace Fabian tell the story of her husband's murder in a video titled *Through It All with Jesus*.[4] One thing impressed me above all else. The Fabians were anything but shallow Christians given to sensationalism. Instead, they were obviously firmly rooted in Scripture.

This impression was further strengthened when I had the privilege of speaking with Grace personally.[5] Instead of being fixated on Satan's power to possess believers, she was focused on God's power to sustain us in the midst of suffering. Far from overestimating the power and province of our adversary, she recognized that God is sovereign over all things, including the temptations of Satan. Through her suffering, Grace came to know ever more fully that nothing can befall us without first passing through the filter of God's love.

In a humble yet convicting manner, Grace emphasized that Satan never had the upper hand—not even the day of her husband's brutal murder. Nor had she or her husband ever entertained the idea that his killer might be a demon-possessed Christian. The very notion was foreign to Grace. Her response to Arnold's account of Edmund's murder was emphatic. "No, no!" she exclaimed. "That's simply not true! I don't know where any of that stuff came from. I hate it when people write and never check their sources."

Furthermore, Grace made it clear that since Arnold had no firsthand knowledge of Edmund's killer, he had no basis on which to determine whether he was demon-possessed. Conversely, Grace, who did have direct contact, stated, "I don't believe that the one who killed my husband is demonized—he is schizophrenic." In fact, said Grace, "When he was transferred from jail to a mental hospital and began to receive medicine for schizophrenia, he became calm, normal, and able to think thoughts about the Lord." She paused for a moment and added, "I know that when he was in the psychiatric ward we would read Scripture to him, and he appeared to be experiencing the grace of God at least then if not before."

Finally, Grace adamantly denied the notion that Edmund's murder had caused Wycliffe "to rethink their position on the relationship of the demonic to believers." In her words, "Our organization has not changed any policy I know of relative to my husband's death in relation to demons. We don't even have a policy on demonization." Wycliffe's U.S. president, Roy Peterson, confirmed that Grace is correct. As he put it, "Our organization had not undertaken any formal review of the relationship of the demonic to believers. If that were the case, Grace would certainly have been aware of it. To use Grace's story in a way she is not familiar with is wrong."[6]

OVERESTIMATING OUR ADVERSARY

Over the years I have read a wide variety of stories that claim to support the notion that Christians can be demon-possessed. In the end they all have one thing in common: They greatly overestimate the power and province of Satan. Some deliverance ministers make a more valiant attempt than others to provide a biblical basis for the contention that Satan can possess believers. Inevitably, however, their experiences and stories overshadow their exegesis of Scripture.

In *The Bondage Breaker,* Dr. Neil Anderson uses in excess of seventy-five (sometimes shocking) stories[7] to demonstrate that 85 percent of all believers are ensnared in some level of satanic bondage. Likewise, in *3 Crucial Questions about Spiritual Warfare,* Arnold seeks to answer the question "Can a Christian be demon-possessed?" by leading off with three extraordinary stories.[8] In addition to a slightly more dramatic version of Edmund Fabian's murder, he employs the story of a woman who was reportedly pinned down and sexually violated by a demon; and the recorded story of a man whose marriage was marvelously saved by Christ but whose demon of rage still causes him to fly off the handle virtually every time he gets into an argument with his wife.

What such stories have in common is that they vastly overrate Satan's power and authority. Sexual demons are the stuff of medieval mythology,[9] and hot-tempered men need to come to grips with the reality that "the devil made me do it" is little more than a convenient cop-out for sin. While it has become fashionable to credit the devil with every temptation we face, we must be ever mindful that spiritual warfare involves the world and the flesh as well. As Paul makes clear in his letter to the Ephesians, we are often defeated in spiritual warfare because we follow "the ways of this world" and "the cravings of our sinful nature" (Ephesians 2:2–3).

To suggest that a Christian can be controlled against his will to such an extent that he murders a fellow believer is the quintessential example of overestimating our adversary. Likewise, the notion that a demon can bite, scrawl on a fogged-up bathroom mirror, or sexually violate a human being has more in common with Greek mythology than a Christian worldview. Concocting "demons of lust," "demons of drugs," or "demons of rage" is at best an example of misplaced emphasis and at worst an illustration of how "the devil made me do it" has become the all-too-prevalent theology of a Christian subculture desperately searching for scapegoats.

In sharp contrast, Christian theology precludes the

possibility of Christians being controlled against their wills through demon-possession. Thus, when Jesus taught his disciples to pray "and lead us not into *temptation,* but deliver us from the evil one," he underscored temptation, rather than demonization, as the means by which the evil one entices us. While deliverance devotees credit the devil for murderous motivations, sexual sensations, and rampant rage, Christ makes it clear that "evil thoughts, murder, adultery, sexual immorality, theft, false testimony, slander," and a host of other sins spring "out of the heart" (Matthew 15:19). The words of the Master echo through the corridors of time with prophetic poignancy: "The good man brings good things out of the good stored up in his heart, and the evil man brings evil things out of the evil stored up in his heart. For out of the overflow of his heart his mouth speaks" (Luke 6:45).

Thus, before the apostle Paul launches into the covering that is our protection in the invisible war, he first warns believers against overestimating the power of Satan by supposing that he can possess and control us against our wills. A proper perspective on spiritual warfare is focused on the power of God, rather than on the ploys of Satan. Says Paul, "Be strong in the Lord and in his mighty power. Put on the full armor of God so that you can take your stand against the devil's schemes" (Ephesians 6:10–11). While our "enemy the devil prowls around like a lion looking for someone to devour" (1 Peter 5:8), he is,

> *A proper perspective on spiritual warfare is focused on the power of God, rather than on the ploys of Satan.*

after all, a lion on a leash the length of which is determined by the Lord.

Two

The Battle for the Mind

For our struggle is not against flesh and blood, but against the rulers,
against the authorities, against the powers of this dark world and
against the spiritual forces of evil in the heavenly realms. Therefore put on
the full armor of God so that when the day of evil comes, you may be able to
stand your ground, and after you have done everything, to stand.
(Ephesians 6:12–13)

One of the things I enjoy most in life is hanging out with my
kids. From the moment I walk through the front door to
the time they hit the sack, they challenge me in everything
from shooting hoops to playing checkers. Often I fall asleep
with the words, "Just one more game!" ringing in my ears.

For years I've had the upper hand. But as my children
continue to grow, the scales have begun to tip in the
opposite direction. My boys now regularly whip me in
basketball, and my girls beat me in checkers more times
than I care to admit. One game I still hold a monopoly
on, however, is golf. In fact, I told my kids that if they ever
beat me in golf, I would put one hundred dollars into
their savings accounts.

The Battle for the Mind

One afternoon the inevitable happened. John Mark, who was only nine at the time, challenged me to a putting contest . . . and won. Johnny's ball had barely reached the bottom of the cup when he looked at me with a mischievous grin and chirped, "Time to pay up, Daddy-O!"

But I was ready for him. "How about double or nothing?" I ventured.

"No way!" Johnny shot back decisively.

"How 'bout I give you a two-shot head start?"

"No!"

"Tell you what I'm going to do. I'll give you a three-shot cushion. Take it or leave it."

By now Johnny was beginning to waiver. "I don't know," he waffled nervously.

"Come on, John Mark, two hundred dollars. I'm giving you three strokes. How are you going to lose a nine-hole putting contest with a three-stroke advantage?" I could see that Johnny was beginning to take the bait. "Yes or no?" I pressed, adding a sense of urgency to my offer.

Reluctantly, Johnny caved in. Ten minutes later he

No matter how enticing the temptation, we are responsible for the choices we make.

was looking up at me with tears in his eyes. "That wasn't fair," he moaned.

"Wasn't fair? What do you mean it wasn't fair? I didn't force you to go double or nothing, did I? It was your choice, wasn't it?"

"Yeah, Dad," Johnny groused. "But you . . . you were just like a temptin' little devil sittin' on my shoulder!"

John Mark was not yet ten, but he learned a life lesson far more valuable than one hundred dollars. Temptation is always crouching at the door. It's as close as a click of your computer mouse and as alluring as easy money. Yet no matter how enticing the temptation, we are responsible for the choices we make. I may have made "the deal" sound too good to pass up, but in the final analysis, it was still Johnny's choice.

Today, John Mark's "temptin' little devil sittin' on my shoulder" quip is a classic. Every time one of us repeats it we all crack up on cue. But there is a serious side: The devil *is* real, and he *does* tempt us in myriad ways. While we greatly overestimate Satan's power by supposing he can control us against our wills, an equal-and-opposite error would be to underestimate his cunning craftiness.

Thus, before Paul launches into the covering that protects against the devil's schemes, he first emphasizes the fact that "our struggle is not against flesh and blood, but against the rulers, against the authorities, against the powers of this dark world and against the spiritual forces of evil in the heavenly realms" (Ephesians 6:12). Spiritual warfare is waged against invisible beings that personify the extremities of evil. And their weapons are spiritual, not physical. While they cannot bite us physically, violate us sexually, or cause us to levitate, they can tempt us to cheat, steal, and lie.

Furthermore, it is crucial to note that though the devil cannot directly interact with us physically, he does have access to our minds. He cannot read our minds, but he can influence our thoughts. Thus, Johnny's "temptin' little devil sittin' on my shoulder" quip was not far from the truth. Indeed, if we open the door to Satan by failing to put on the full armor of God, he does, as it were, sit on our shoulders and whisper into our ears. The whisper cannot be discerned with the physical ear; it can, however, penetrate "the ear" of the mind.

We cannot explain how such communication takes place any more than we can explain how our minds can cause the physical synapses of the brain to fire. But that such mind-to-mind communication takes place is indisputable. If it were not so, the devil could not have tempted Judas to betray his Master, seduced Ananias and Sapphira to deceive Peter, or incited David to take a census. Nor would the apostle Paul have instructed us to "put on the full armor of God, so that when the day of evil comes, you may be able to stand your ground, and after you have done everything, to stand" (Ephesians 6:13). In the final analysis, the whole of Scripture informs us that spiritual warfare is the battle for the mind.

Finally, Paul wants us to understand that while fallen angels are not physical beings, they are as real as the very flesh upon our bones. They are malevolent beings, the vastness of whose intellect exceeds that of any human who has ever lived. Thus, "we must not expect that a man, unaided from above, should ever be a match for an angel, especially an angel whose intellect has been sharpened by malice."[1] From the Garden of Eden to the present generation, Satan and the hordes of hell have honed the craft of temptation.

No doubt much to his delight, we often depict the devil as either a cartoonish clown—with an elongated tail, red tights, and a pitchfork—or as a cultural caricature that traces "strange symbols" on bathroom mirrors, warns a Christian leader with "two little bite-marks," or pillages a woman by "violating her sexually." Far from silly or stupid, Satan appears as a cosmopolitan angel of enlightenment. In the words of C. S. Lewis, "The greatest evil is not now done in those sordid 'dens of crime' that Dickens loved to paint. It is not done even in concentration camps and labour camps. In those we see its final result. But is conceived and ordered (moved, seconded, carried, and minuted) in clean, carpeted, warmed, and well-lighted offices, by quiet men with white collars and cut fingernails and smooth-shaven cheeks, who do not need to raise their voices."[2]

Rather than brutish, demons are brilliant. As Randy Alcorn notes, "They operate within a hierarchy dependent on issuing, receiving, and carrying out orders. They wage war against God, righteous angels, and us. Intelligence gathering, strategy, deploying troops, communicating battle orders, and reporting on the results of engagements are all fundamental aspects of warfare. . . . They live in a spiritual world where there's a certain clarity of thought even among the fallen. . . . Their modus operandi is to twist, deceive, and mislead, but they are intimately familiar with the truth they twist."[3]

While contemporary Christians are fixating on seven step programs by people such as Frank and Ida Mae Hammond (Pigs in the Parlor), they have all but forgotten the seven steps to freedom presented in Scripture by the Apostle Paul. Satan knows full well that without the spiritual armor listed by Paul in Ephesians 6, we are but pawns in the devil's game. Little wonder then that since the days of the Puritans, precious little that is worthwhile has been written concerning the full armor of God.

THREE

The Covering of Truth

Stand firm then, with the belt of truth buckled around your waist.
(Ephesians 6:14)

Imagine traveling back in time to the late 1970s. As you are sitting in church on Sunday morning, your pastor announces that next week the church will be hosting a special conference with a former Satanist who has been miraculously transformed by the power of the gospel.

You can hardly believe your ears. This is precisely what you have been waiting for. For months now you have been trying to convince a neighbor who dabbles in the occult that Satanism poses incredible dangers. But so far your efforts have been to no avail. So you rush home and invite him to church. While your neighbor has labeled you a "naive fundamentalist," he won't be able to say that about a genuine ex-Satanist.

The next weekend quickly arrives, and you are seated

next to your neighbor in church. John Todd is introduced as a former Satanist, a courier for the satanic ruling council, the Illuminati. He is now a brother in Christ, free from the shackles of satanic power.

Todd opens his message with a bang. According to him, few people have any idea how powerful and pervasive Satanism really is. Movies such as *The Exorcist* and *Rosemary's Baby* are just the tip of a very insidious iceberg. The real danger, he thinks, lies in a carefully crafted cartel encompassing policemen, politicians, and even pastors who are secretly engaged in subterfuge to advance their satanic agenda—an agenda that has moved Satanism into the very halls of power as well as into the sanctuaries of religion. Todd ought to know, because as a courier for the Illuminati, he personally made payoffs to dozens of prominent people, including Christian leaders. *No* organization—including the church—is immune from infiltration.

Immediately images begin to flash in rapid succession in your mind. You wonder if Todd might be referring to an evangelist you saw begging for money on television just last night. Or maybe it's a local Mormon bishop who chairs your community's ecumenical council?

Three words, however, snap you back to reality: "Pastor Chuck Smith." In stunned disbelief you hear Todd insinuate that Chuck Smith, the founder of the Calvary Chapel movement, is a secret Satanist. He has been strategically situated by Satan to seduce young people by imprisoning their minds with secular tunes sung to deceptively innocuous lyrics masking subliminal satanic messages.

You cannot—you will not—believe that one of the catalysts for the Jesus movement is in reality a pawn in the hands of Beelzebub. As though anticipating your thoughts, Todd reminds his audience that Satan seldom uses obvious candidates for his deadly deceptions because he knows they won't be believed. Rather, Todd says that he uses those noted for piety and honesty. Besides Todd knows firsthand. He was there. As a courier for the Illuminati, he personally delivered a total of eight million dollars to Chuck Smith. The instructions he passed on to Chuck were to start Maranatha Music and use it to pervert the minds of unsuspecting converts.

Still, you find this hard to swallow. How could anyone who names the name of Christ so blatantly betray his Lord? Todd seems to have a ready answer for everything. Judas betrayed the Lord for only thirty pieces of silver. Why would anyone think it is far-fetched for Chuck Smith to betray Christ for eight million dollars?

Nervously, you sneak a peek at your neighbor. To your amazement, he doesn't appear to be the least bit skeptical. His eyes are riveted on Todd. It's as though Todd and he are the only people in the sanctuary. As Todd transitions into his altar call, your friend rushes forward and without hesitation gives his heart to the Lord. Whatever doubts you still harbor instantly vaporize. Todd *must* be right—just look at the fruit!

Jump forward with me from the late 1970s to the present. John Todd no longer preaches. He has lost his popularity in a plunge from pulpit to prison—a convicted felon, an exposed deceiver. And your neighbor? Sadly, his faith was short-lived. The last time you ran into him, he shoved a newspaper account of Todd's conviction under your nose. "Why should I follow your Christ?" he bellowed. "You Christians are all alike. If truth was really on your side, you wouldn't have to concoct stories to scare people into believing!"[1]

TRUTH TWISTERS

Like John Todd, former Christian megastar Mike Warnke introduces himself as "an ex-Satanist high priest, who ran more than fifteen hundred members of 'The Brotherhood' in Southern California." As an insider of the Illuminati, Satanism's premier governing body, Warnke purportedly "reveals the whole grisly—and frightening—truth" about Satanism.[2] His book *The Satan Seller* purports to tell the story of how "a clean-cut, churchgoing, college freshman" "got sucked into booze, drugs, group sex parties" and the obligatory "Black Masses" of Satanism.[3] "The Brotherhood" pleasured him with everything from "gorgeous drapes" to "two chicks sitting on a white rug."[4] And his "Black Masses" were replete with animal sacrifices and "nude-adorned" altars.[5]

As it turns out, such voyeuristic tales sprang from little more than a fertile imagination.[6] In a make-believe world, Warnke gained power, sex, and money as a servant of Satan; in the real world, he achieved the world, the flesh, and the devil under the guise of serving his Savior.

Like *The Satan Seller,* Lauren Strafford's Christian best-seller *Satan's Underground* became "one of the key sources for promoting, perpetuating, and validating the satanic ritual abuse (SRA), 'adult survivor' and 'repressed memories' hysteria that peaked in the early 1990s."[7] Details and documentation, however, demonstrate that Lauren Stratford is, in reality, "Laurel Rose Willson, a troubled woman from Washington State who spent most of her teen and adult life fabricating horrendous stories of victimization by a variety of people in a variety of settings."[8]

After her pornographic tales of satanic ritual abuse were exposed as fabrications, Laurel Willson simply rein-vented herself as Laura Grabowski, a Jewish Holocaust survivor. "Before she pointed to the scars of her self-mutilation as the work of her abusive parent(s), the pornographers, or the Satanists; now she points to the scars on her arms and whispers, 'Mengele's child,' the work of Dr. Mengele and his medical experiments."[9]

Those who disbelieve her story are dubbed pawns in a vast satanic conspiracy.

Unfortunately, such stories are not anomalies. Under the guise of truth, Christians have communicated the legend of Darwin's deathbed conversion;[10] boycotted Procter & Gamble because its president allegedly confessed his company's ties to Satanism;[11] defended the historicity of the Gospels through such well-known forgeries as the Pilate letter;[12] argued for the inspiration of Scripture on the basis of imbedded Bible codes;[13] told the tale of James Bartley, who was supposedly swallowed by a whale, to substantiate the biblical account of Jonah;[14] circulated the story of scientists discovering hell in Siberia to support the Bible's teachings concerning eternal conscious torment;[15] perpetuated the urban legend that NASA discovered Joshua's "Lost Day";[16] and employed sloppy journalism to circulate an endless variety of resurrection stories.[17]

As Os Guinness chronicles in *Time for Truth,* such creative storytelling is pandemic in the broader culture as well. It runs the gamut from "NBC television's staged report on the exploding General Motors trucks, later acknowledged to be planted detonations" to "Norma McCorvey's (AKA Jane Roe) fabricated story of rape, encouraged by proabortion leaders, that was so instrumental in the U. S. Supreme Court's 1973 decision, *Roe v. Wade*."[18] Such truth-twisting tactics are inevitably justified by the "Larger Truth that filmmaker Oliver Stone used in defending the facts in one of his films: 'Even if I'm totally wrong . . . I am still right . . . I am essentially right because I am depicting the Evil with a capital E.'"[19]

WHAT IS TRUTH?

In an age in which Internet fabrications "travel halfway around the world before truth has had a chance to put its boots on,"[20] Paul's words ring through the centuries with added urgency: "Stand firm then, with the belt of truth buckled around your waist" (Ephesians 6:14). As your waist is the center of your body, so truth is central to the full armor of God. Without it, the covering that protects you from the devil's schemes simply crumples to the ground, leaving you naked and vulnerable.

But what is truth? This is the very question Pontius Pilate asked Jesus (see John 18:38). In the irony of the ages he stood toe-to-toe with the personification of truth and yet missed its reality. Postmodern people are in much the same position. They stare at truth but fail to recognize its identity.

Truth, like all the other pieces of the armor, is in actuality an aspect of the nature of God himself.[21] Thus to put on the belt of truth is to put on Christ. For Christ is "truth" (John 14:6), and Christians are the bearers of truth. As Os Guinness explains, Christianity is not true because it works (pragmatism); it is not true because it feels right (subjectivism); it is not true because it's "my truth" (relativism). It is true because it is anchored in the person of Christ. "The Christian faith is not true because it works; it works because it is true. It is not true because we experience it; we experience it—deeply and gloriously—because it is true. It is not simply 'true for us'; it is true for any who seek in order to find, because truth is true even if nobody believes it, and falsehood is false even if everybody believes it. That is why truth does not yield to opinion, fashion, numbers, office, or sincerity—it is simply true and that is the end of it."[22]

Furthermore, truth is essential to a realistic world-view. The moment we drop 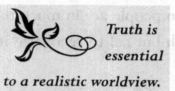 the belt of truth, our view of reality becomes seriously skewed. Todd's conspiracy theories, Warnke's voyeuristic tales, and Stratford's repressed memories of satanic ritual abuse evolve out of sophistry, sensationalism, and superstition, as do Larson's sexual demons, Anderson's biting demons, and Arnold's demons of death.

Truth is essential to a realistic worldview.

No doubt Satan is as pleased with ministers who insinuate that demons "are but literary symbols of man's inhumanity to man"[23] as he is with those whose demonology is driven by Hollywood stereotypes. In Randy Alcorn's book *Lord Foulgrin's Letters,* Lord Foulgrin instructs his demonic understudy Squaltaint that "we can benefit immensely from any view of us but the true one. Probe carefully to discover your patient's demonology and develop it in the most advantageous manner. Make sure his view of us stems from skepticism, denial, ignorance, superstition, legend, literature, spiritism, popular culture, or any combination thereof. Let it come from anything and everything but the forbidden book."[24]

Finally, dropping the belt of truth is fraught with peril. If you think you have been exorcised from "the demon of bulimia," you will think you have discovered a fast-food solution to a long-term problem. If you believe you have been delivered from the demon of cancer, you will believe you no longer need medical intervention. And if you suppose you have delivered someone from "the demon of murder," you will suppose that the person is no longer a threat to himself or society.

Think back for a moment to the murder of Edmund Fabian. As documented by Grace, her husband's killer was a textbook schizophrenic. When he was on medication, he was calm and lucid. When he was not, the voices in his head returned.

Imagine what might have happened if someone supposed that Edmund's killer was satanically possessed, as opposed to schizophrenically psychotic. Imagine that the remedy of choice was deliverance, rather than medication. Suppose that after the exorcism, the killer was no longer considered a menace to society. After all, he had been delivered of the demon that made him do it.

Imagine further that the court disagreed with the Christian exorcists and diagnosed Edmund's killer with schizophrenic psychosis, rather than satanic possession. Imagine he was put on medication and released back into society. Now imagine the unimaginable. Imagine Edmund's killer stopped taking his medication, the voices returned, and once again he had blood on his hands.

Now stop imagining! Edmund's killer was indeed released into the village. He stopped controlling his psychotic breaks through medication. The voices in his head returned, and he took another life. This time it was his own.[25]

Indeed the belt of truth is essential to a realistic world-view. When its buckle breaks, the covering crumples. Reality is clouded. The unthinkable happens.

FOUR

The Covering of Righteousness

Stand firm then . . . with the breastplate of righteousness in place.
(Ephesians 6:14)

Would that the question had been, "Can the Catholic Church help save society?" Instead, in large letters superimposed over the image of a shamed priest, the question was, "Can the Catholic Church save itself?" *Time's* April 1, 2002, cover story chronicled an epidemic of sexual abuse and official cover-ups that has shaken the Roman Catholic Church to its very core. Worse yet, the sexual practices of predatory priests have cast an ominous shadow over Christianity itself. Their behavior has shattered lives, destroyed trust, and marginalized the credibility of the church.

Little wonder then that Paul urges us to "stand firm . . . with the breastplate of righteousness in place" (Ephesians 6:14). Truth without righteousness is abhorrent. No matter how correct our worldview, or resplendent our orthodoxy, if it is not coupled with righteousness, we forfeit the moral authority to speak. In the words of Puritan writer William Gurnall, "An orthodox judgment coming from an unholy heart and an ungodly life is as ugly as a man's head would be on a beast's shoulders. The wretch who knows the truth but practices evil is worse than the man who is ignorant."[1]

It would have been inconceivable for a Roman soldier to engage a physical enemy without a breastplate. Likewise, it is foolhardy to engage the enemy of our souls without the breastplate of righteousness firmly in place. As a breastplate or a bullet-proof vest is a physical heart protector, so the breastplate of righteousness is a spiritual heart protector. Without it we are impotent in the invisible war.

Righteousness is the core of Christianity compressed into a single word.

Righteousness is the core of Christianity compressed into a single word. The forces of darkness are bent on frustrating it. The "bright Morning Star" (Revelation 22:16) came to fulfill it. Righteousness is what the Book of Romans is all about. In fact, it might well be retitled "the breastplate of righteousness," for in it the gospel of "righteousness from God is revealed, a righteousness that is by faith from first to last" (Romans 1:17). This is the righteousness "to which the Law and the Prophets testify" (Romans 3:21). And "this righteousness from God comes through faith in Jesus Christ to all who believe" (Romans 3:22).

First and foremost, the breastplate of righteousness protects against self-righteousness. Scripture likens self-righteousness to "filthy rags" (Isaiah 64:6). Every single religious construct outside of Christianity is based on self-righteous attempts to become good enough for God. Romans, however, refutes religious remedies by teaching that "God credits righteousness *apart* from works" (Romans 4:6; emphasis added). What Martin Luther described as "the gate to heaven" is summarized in the words, "The just shall live by faith alone" (cf. Romans 1:17; cf. 3:28).

Paul begins Romans by depicting the chasm between God and man: "For all have sinned and fall short of the glory of God" (Romans 3:23). He proceeds by declaring that the chasm between our sin and God's righteousness cannot be bridged by observing the law. "We maintain that a man is justified by faith apart from observing the law" (Romans 3:28). He concludes by demonstrating that Abraham's faith was "credited to him as righteousness" (Romans 4:9). And adds Paul, "The words 'it was credited to him' were written not for him alone, but also for us, to whom God will credit righteousness—for us who believe in him who raised Jesus our Lord from the dead" (Romans 4:23–24).

Furthermore, we put on righteousness as a breast-plate by becoming slaves to righteousness. Says Paul, "Thanks be to God that, though you used to be slaves to sin, you wholeheartedly obeyed the form of teaching to which you were entrusted. You have been set free from sin and have become slaves to righteousness. I put this in human terms because you are weak in your natural selves. Just as you used to offer the parts of your body in slavery to impurity and to ever-increasing wickedness, so now offer them in slavery to righteousness leading to holiness" (Romans 6:17–19).

Those who wish to emulate Tiger Woods do not become Tigerlike by simply donning a Nike Swoosh, nor do they win the Grand Slam of golf by merely droning Nike's "Just do it" slogan. Instead, they become Tigerlike through mental and physical discipline. Similarly, those who wish to emulate Jesus Christ do not

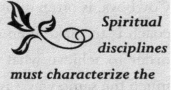

Spiritual disciplines must characterize the lives of those who sincerely desire to become Christlike.

become Christlike by simply taking on the appearance of Christianity, nor do they win the good fight by merely mouthing Christian slogans. Instead, they become Christlike by offering themselves to God "as living sacrifices" (Romans 12:1). Prayer, fasting, and sacrifice characterized the life of Christ. In like fashion, such spiritual disciplines must characterize the lives of those who sincerely desire to become Christlike.

Spiritual disciplines are, in effect, spiritual exercises. As the physical disciplines of weightlifting and running promote strength and stamina, so the spiritual disciplines of abstinence (solitude, sacrifice, simplicity, etc.) and engagement (study, service, submission, etc.) promote righteousness.[2] Tom Landry, former coach of the Dallas

Cowboys, is often quoted as saying, "The job of a football coach is to make men do what they don't want to do in order to achieve what they've always wanted to be."[3] In much the same way, says Donald Whitney, "Christians are called to make themselves do something they would not naturally do—pursue the Spiritual Disciplines—in order to become what they've always wanted to be, that is, like Jesus Christ."[4]

The problem with contemporary Christianity is that a vast majority of Christians have never made the transition from declaration to discipleship. Thus, they have never become slaves to righteousness. Dietrich Bonhoeffer was right in debunking easy-believism in *The Cost of Discipleship*. However, as noted by Dallas Willard, "the cost of nondiscipleship is far greater."[5]

To neglect discipleship and spiritual disciplines for deliverance and sensual distractions is to give birth to an unholy church. Such a church "is of no use to the world and of no esteem among men. . . . It is an abomination, hell's laughter, heaven's abhorrence. And the larger the church, the more influential, the worse nuisance it becomes when it becomes unholy. The worst evils which have ever come upon the world have been brought upon her by an unholy church."[6]

In C. S. Lewis's *The Screwtape Letters,* Uncle Screwtape is displeased with Wormwood because his patient has become a Christian. However, says Screwtape, "There is no need to despair: Hundreds of these adult converts have been reclaimed after a brief sojourn in the Enemy's camp and are now with us. All the *habits* of the patient, both mental and bodily, are still in our favour."[7] Screwtape knew full well that converts who failed to embrace spiritual discipline and discipleship would likewise fail to become Christlike. Put another way, unless and until a convert becomes a slave to righteousness, there is no need for the forces of darkness to be alarmed.

Finally, to put on the breastplate of righteousness is to reject superstitious righteousness. Superstitious righteousness does not trouble the tempter in the least. Why should it? After all, the most powerful weapon in Satan's arsenal is subterfuge. He is pleased to have us presume that possessing our bodies is his greatest achievement, when in reality, it is our righteousness he covets most. From the creation of man until the present day, Satan's purpose has been to strip us of our armor and to rob us of our righteousness.

In all the ways Satan sought to pillage Job, he never petitioned God to possess his body. As William Gurnall points out, it was not pity that influenced Satan; "he was holding out for higher stakes, hoping to possess Job's soul. It would have been a thousand times more satisfying if Job himself had blasphemed God (rather than the devil, having possessed Job's body, belching out curses through him). That would have been Job's sin, not Satan's."[8]

The tragedy today is that multitudes suppose that righteousness can be achieved through deliverance, rather than through discipleship. Thus, Christians who struggle with lust are said to be possessed by the "demon of lust," and deliverance is said to be "the key to moral and psychological redemption." Everything from rampant substance addiction to a runaway sexual appetite is pawned off on demons, with the added bonus that

Christians are no longer held personally responsible for sin. Indwelling demons are said to be the problem, and getting rid of them is said to be the secret to restoring righteousness.

Randy Alcorn cleverly underscores the problem of superstitious righteousness in a communiqué from Lord Foulgrin to his demonic understudy Squaltaint:

My beloved Squaltaint,

Make the vermin ignore us when we're there, and exorcise us when we aren't. Let them lay hands on people and cast out the demon of loneliness, the demon of back pain, the demon of kidney stones, and the demon of constipation. Not only is this a distraction from our central work, on their minds and morals, it has a bonus—because of their silliness, others conclude "all this demon stuff is nonsense."

When they ponder demon activity, make Bible believers think, "Back then, but not now; over there, but not here." Let the gulf of time and distance convince them they're somehow beyond the cosmic war.

I'm pleased when the squadrons teach them nothing about us, and when they teach error and excess about us. Let them see us behind every bush or behind no bush at all. Let them see us in every convulsion, handicap, foaming at the mouth, gnashing of teeth, or display of superhuman strength. Or let them see us in none of them. Let them fear we're everywhere or imagine we're nowhere. Psychological and medical labels are easy to hide behind. "Multiple personality disorder?" Been there. Done that.

Fortunately, many of these spiritual warfare experts don't know what they're doing, even when they publish how-to manuals on casting us out. I don't minimize the horror of sudden eviction. It's humiliating and unnerving. The first time it happened, all I could think of was the Enemy casting me into the nether darkness before my time.

But even if the expulsion works, it leaves a vacuum. How will they fill it? Let them cast us out, or imagine they have, as long as the vermin keep making the daily choices that invite us back in. Let them "name" and "bind" us to their hearts' content, as long as they enter-tain the thoughts and engage in the activities that give us power over them.

Make them think we can control them against their will, or, because they're Christians, we can't influence them at all. Both lies are useful. If they never think about us, we have them. If they always think about us, we have them. Ignore us, they're ours. Obsess over us, they're ours. Having their eyes on us is as good as having them on themselves. The only important thing is, they don't have them on Him.

The Book doesn't tell them to rebuke a spirit of dissension, but to agree and be united in the same mind. It doesn't tell them to rebuke a demon of incest, but that the offender must repent and change his behavior or be expelled.

We can short-circuit discipleship by telling them they can break patterns of sin simply by uttering magic words requiring no ongoing acts of obedience. Who needs accountability and discipline to establish new patterns of purity when they can simply cast out the demon of lust? . . . I've been in deliverance encounters where I've fed them a steady stream of false information. You can't imagine how many of them believe what I say, even when they've rebuked me as a "lying spirit"! I saw an entire chapter of a book conveying information I gave them——nearly all of it I just made up while they tried to exorcise me! Did somebody say "gullible"?

. . . It's not power plays and sweeping declarations of our defeat that frighten me, it's quiet prayers for personal holiness and greater yieldedness to the Enemy. Far better that they focus on us than look to their own hearts or ask the Enemy to cleanse them. . . .

Never frightened by their grandstanding,
—Lord Foulgrin[9]

Examine yourself. Do you suffer from self-righteousness? Put on the breastplate of righteousness by embracing the Savior's righteousness. Have you become a slave to righteousness or are you still a slave to sin? Put on the breastplate of righteousness by practicing the spiritual disciplines. Is your righteousness based on superstition, rather than Scripture? Put on the breastplate of righteousness by shifting your focus from deliverance to discipleship. We must ever be mindful that righteousness, like truth, is rooted in the very nature of God. As God puts on "righteousness as his breastplate" (Isaiah 59:17), God's representatives are to reflect that righteousness in our daily lives.

The tragedy today is that multitudes suppose that righteousness can be achieved through deliverance, rather than through discipleship.

FIVE

The Covering of Peace

*Stand firm . . . with your feet fitted with the readiness
that comes from the gospel of peace.* (Ephesians 6:15)

As I begin this chapter, the National Basketball Association's second season—the NBA playoffs—are in full swing. This year the world-champion Los Angeles Lakers are odds-on favorites to win the basketball wars for a third straight year. Not only do they feature Kobe Bryant, widely touted as the heir apparent to Michael Jordan, but they boast Shaquille O'Neal, arguably the most dominant "big man" in the history of the NBA. One obstacle stands between the Lakers and a three-peat, however—Shaq's arthritic big toe. Despite Shaq's strength and skill, a tiny foot problem threatens to bring the game's big man down to size.

Much as he hates to admit it, when his toes ache, Shaq doesn't have the same quickness to the ball, can't block as many shots, and isn't as Godzillalike on the glass. Thus, to prepare him for battle, Shaq's size twenty-twos have been fitted with a special pair of sneakers complete with a technologically advanced carbon orthotic device. No expense was spared because, if Shaq can't stand, the Lakers will fall.

As Shaq's sneakers are essential to winning the basketball wars, so too our feet must be properly fitted in order to prevail in spiritual warfare. All the skill and resources humanity has to offer have been brought to bear on protecting the feet of a thirty-million-dollar-per-year basketball star. That, however, pales by comparison to the price that was paid to have our "feet fitted with the readiness that comes from the gospel of peace."

In the eloquent words of Charles Haddon Spurgeon, the prince of preachers: "We believe in a gospel that was formed in the purpose of God from all eternity, designed with infinite wisdom, wrought out at an enormous expense, costing nothing less than the blood of Jesus, brought home by the infinite power of the Holy Spirit; a gospel full of blessings, any one of which would outweigh a world in price; a gospel as free as it is full; a gospel everlasting and immutable; gospel of which we can never think too much, whose praises we can never exaggerate!"[1]

Spurgeon went on to say that from this gospel "its choicest essence is taken—namely, its peace—and from this peace those sandals are prepared with which a man may tread on the lion and the adder, and even on the fierce burning coals of malice, slander, and persecution."[2] Indeed, the priceless material with which God has fitted our feet for readiness in the battle "against the rulers, against the authorities, against the powers of this dark world, and against the spiritual forces of evil in the heavenly realms" is nothing less than the gospel of peace (Ephesians 6:12).

Paul's emphasis here first and foremost is peace with God. "Once you were alienated from God and were enemies in your minds because of your evil behavior" (Colossians 1:21). Once your heart entertained contemptible thoughts about God. You had an inbred disgust for his principles and precepts. Your will was at odds with his will. And under the banner of Satan, you openly engaged in warfare with God. "But now he has reconciled you by Christ's physical body through death to present you holy in his sight, without blemish and free from accusation" (Colossians 1:22).

Thus, as soldiers of the cross, we can march through life's battles with a song in our hearts and 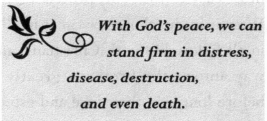 *With God's peace, we can stand firm in distress, disease, destruction, and even death.* with our feet fitted with the readiness that comes from the gospel of peace. God does not promise us a panacea, but he does promise us peace in the midst of life's storms. With God's peace, we can stand firm in distress, disease, destruction, and even death. For when our burden of sin has been removed, all other burdens become bearable. And we can stand firm in the assurance that "the God of peace will soon crush Satan under [our] feet" (Romans 16:20).

Furthermore, to stand firm with our feet fitted with the readiness that comes from the gospel of peace is to have peace with others. While we cannot make everyone love us, we can love everyone. Fitted with the gospel of peace, we can tread confidently through conflict and controversy with other Christians. Says Spurgeon, "An unwillingness to think badly of any Christian is a sandal most easy to the foot, protecting it from many a thorn. Wear it in the church, wear it in all holy service, wear it in all fellowship with Christians, and you will find your way among the brethren greatly smoothed. You will before long win their love and esteem and avoid a world of jealousy and opposition that would otherwise have impeded your course."[3]

The priceless covering with which our feet are fitted even affords peace with those who are yet unconverted. Says Solomon, "When a man's ways are pleasing to the LORD, he makes even his enemies to live at peace with him" (Proverbs 16:7). Put another way, submission to God and a life beyond reproach will disarm your adversaries. As Peter promises, addressing the world with a clear conscience will cause "those who speak maliciously against your good behavior in Christ" to be "ashamed of their slander" (1 Peter 3:16).

Finally, the gospel of peace is a preview of the promise of perfect peace in paradise. In the present, peace is yet unperfected. But as soldiers of the cross we continue on toward the promise, and one day we will step over the threshold into perfect peace. Gurnall likens our present condition to a budding flower in springtime. "On a warm day it opens a little, but as the cold night comes its petals shut tightly again." Likewise, though there are now times of "love and peace among Christians, differences arise which drive back the sweet spring. But in heaven it is full blown and continues that way throughout eternity. Not only is the wound of contention healed; a scar is not to be seen on the face of heaven's peace to disfigure its beauty."[4] The bottom line is this: Believers who stand firm with their feet fitted with the readiness that comes from the gospel of peace are only a step away from perfect peace. For as Paul puts it, those he justified he also glorified (see Romans 8:30).

What shoes are to our feet, spiritual readiness is to our souls. When Shaq's feet are properly fitted, he stands strong in the basketball wars. Without his special sneakers, however, he dares not step out into the battle. So too it is with the Christian in spiritual warfare. With peace in our souls, we are spiritually ready to face all the trials and tribulations life brings our way.

Horatio Spafford personified such readiness when he penned the words, *"When peace, like a river, attendeth my way, when sorrows like sea billows roll; whatever my lot thou hast taught me to say, "It is well, it is well with my soul."* More profound than even the words themselves is the context in which they were written. Spafford's son had recently died. His real estate investments had been obliterated in the Chicago Fire of 1871. And his daughters Bessie, Annie, Maggie, and Tanetta had drowned in the Atlantic Ocean after the *S.S. Villa du Havre* had been broadsided by an English vessel.

Yet in the midst of the rolling sea billows that stole his prized possessions, the words continued to spill forth from a broken heart. *"Though Satan should buffet, though trials should come, let this blest assurance control, that Christ has regarded my helpless estate, and has shed his own blood for my soul."*

These were not the words of a man who believed that Christ was a mere magical mantra that would make his pain go away. No, these were the words of a man who had experienced peace with God, and peace with others. Thus enabled, he continued, *"My sin——O the bliss of this glorious thought!——my sin, not in part but the whole, is nailed to the cross and I bear it no more; praise the Lord, praise the Lord, O my soul!"*

And still he was not done. With feet fitted with the readiness that comes from the gospel of peace he looked forward to the prospect of perfect peace in paradise. So inspired, he finished his hymn with these words:

O Lord, haste the day when the faith shall be sight,
the clouds be rolled back as a scroll,
the trump shall resound and the Lord shall descend,
'Even so'——it is well with my soul."

Six

The Covering of Faith

In addition to all this, take up the shield of faith,
with which you can extinguish all the flaming arrows
of the evil one. (Ephesians 6:16)

Long before the advent of extreme sports, there was extreme faith. Indeed, the Book of Job might well be dubbed "Extreme Faith," for in its pages Job experienced the ultimate test of faith. Job endured more tragedy in a single day than most people experience in an entire lifetime. In the span of a few hours his servants were slaughtered, his possessions were stolen, and his children perished in a collapsing house. And that was only the beginning. Within days his body was covered "with painful sores from the soles of his feet to the top of his head" (Job 2:7). His wife turned against him, snarling, "Curse God and die!" (v. 9). And his "friends" attacked him with a series of insufferable speeches. "Surely God does not reject a blameless man," they taunted (Job 8:20).

Unbeknownst to Job, he was the subject of an extreme test of faith. God affirmed Job's faith as firm and faultless; Satan assailed Job's faith as fickle and fleeting. "Stretch out your hand and strike everything he has," Satan hissed to God, "and he will surely curse you to your face" (Job 1:11). In the cosmic contest that ensued, Job responded with remarkable resolve. Emotionally, he was on a roller coaster, his mind desperately searching for answers. Yet in the end Job personified extreme faith by staking his fate and fortune on the trustworthiness of God. His eternal perspective is forever enshrined in the words, "Though he slay me, yet will I hope in him" (Job 13:15).

With the shield of faith in hand, Job was enabled to stand strong and steadfast against persecutions, temptations, and even the blasphemous thoughts Satan whispered in his ear. When all was said and done, the sinister serpent was able to scorch Job's shield but unable to sear his soul. Little wonder, then, that in addition to truth, righteousness, and peace, Paul urges us to "take up the shield of faith, with which you can extinguish all the flaming arrows of the evil one" (Ephesians 6:16).

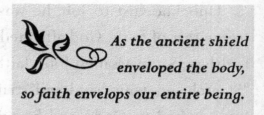

As the ancient shield enveloped the body, so faith envelops our entire being.

As the ancient shield enveloped the body, so faith envelops our entire being. When Satan attacks our heads, the hand of faith holds fast to truth. When Satan attacks our hearts, the hand of faith holds fast to righteousness. In fact, it might well be said that the shield of faith is the apex of the Christian's armor. It is the covering that protects not only the entirety of our bodies, but all the other pieces of the armor as well.

Faith is a defense for all defenses. Every other piece of the full armor of God must inevitably operate in conjunction with faith. In the words of William Gurnall, "Faith is armour upon armour, a grace that preserves all the other graces."[1] In ancient warfare, "the shield was prized by a soldier above all other pieces of armor. He counted it a greater shame to lose his shield than to lose the battle; and therefore he would not part with it even when he was under the very foot of the enemy, but esteemed it an honor to die with his shield in his hand."[2]

Faith is ultimately rooted and grounded in the nature of God himself. And nothing is more crucial to Christianity than a proper understanding of who God is. In Christian theology he is portrayed as the Sovereign of the universe. He is described as spirit, perfectly wise, self-sufficient, omnipotent, and omniscient. The Bible depicts him as the one who sees all and knows all from all eternity, the one who wields supreme and absolute authority. Thus, in biblical vernacular, faith is a *channel of living trust*—an assurance—that stretches from man to God. In other words, it is the object of faith that renders faith faithful.

Indeed, the greatest demonstration of faith is trusting God even when we do not understand. It is the sort of confidence exemplified by Job as he persevered in the midst of affliction, trusting God despite the whirlwind that threatened to blow his life into oblivion. Likewise, it is the trait most demonstrated in the life of the apostle Paul, who not only fought the good fight, but also finished the race and kept his faith. His faith, like that of

Job, was not fixed on his temporary circumstances, but on the trustworthiness of his Creator.

The Faith Hall of Fame in Hebrews 11 is filled with men and women who trusted God even when they did not understand. Those who like Gideon, Barak, Samson, Jephthah, David, Samuel, and the prophets through faith conquered kingdoms; who have been tortured, jeered, and flogged; who have been chained and put in prison; stoned and put to death; destitute; persecuted and mistreated, yet were commended for their faith—because their faith was fixed on God.[3]

Furthermore, the shield of faith is preeminent among the graces because it is forged from the finished work of Christ. Indeed it may well be said that the shield of faith is fashioned from the blood-red fabric of Christ's righteousness. For the spotless robes of Christ's righteousness replace the filthy robes of our self-righteousness and give us the right to refer to God as "our Father." As Paul explains in Romans 8, those who are led by the Spirit of God are no longer illegitimate children. Instead, they too are sons and daughters by adoption through faith in Jesus.

Says Gurnall, "Faith has two hands. With one it pulls off its own righteousness and throws it away, as David discarded Saul's armour; with the other it puts on Christ's righteousness to cover the soul's shame."[4]

The faith that serves to protect us in spiritual warfare is not to be confused with mere knowledge. Millions worldwide believe in the trustworthiness of Billy Graham. They have heard him proclaim the good news on television and yet do not believe that his message corresponds to reality. Thus, they have the knowledge that it takes to be saved but do not have saving faith. Others hear the message, agree that it corresponds to reality, but due to the hardness of their hearts do not bow. Rather, like the demons, they continue to live in fearful anticipation of the judgment to come (see James 2:19). Some, however, have what Scripture describes as genuine justifying faith—a faith that not only knows about the gospel and agrees that its content corresponds to reality, but a faith by which they are transformed.

People with pneumonia may know about penicillin. They may even agree that penicillin has saved millions. But until they receive it, they demonstrate that they do not genuinely believe in it. In like fashion, only those who receive the regal robes of Christ's righteousness are redeemed. Christ's righteousness is the covering; faith is the hand that puts it on.

Christ's righteousness is the covering; faith is the hand that puts it on.

Finally, the shield of faith is of paramount importance because it is the grace "with which you can extinguish *all* the flaming arrows of the evil one" (Ephesians 6:16; emphasis added). This is not an uncertain promise. Rather, it is divine assurance that faith equips us to escape the very extremities of evil. Says John, "This is the victory that has overcome the world, even our faith" (1 John 5:4).

The world fuels an unholy trinity—"the cravings of sinful man, the lust of the eyes and the boasting of what he has and does" (1 John 2:16). The shield of faith, however, extinguishes the flames. Faith focuses on the permanent pleasures of paradise rather than pseudo-pleasures of the present; it blinds the unclean eye that

74

lusts after pornography or wealth; and it deadens the pride of life that covets "praise from men more than praise from God" (John 12:43).

The eye of faith looks at life with eternity in mind. It looks back to Job, who blazed a trail of faith for all God's people who would follow. And it looks forward to the promise of eternity when temptations will be no more. The tempter will be thrown into the lake of burning sulfur, and we will enter the golden city with divine assurance that "nothing impure will ever enter it, nor will anyone who does what is shameful or deceitful, but only those whose names are written in the Lamb's book of life" (Revelation 21:27).

In the meantime, we can rest assured that in the sovereign plan of God even the flaming arrows of the evil one are being forged into instruments by which the fabric of our faith is woven into an exquisite tapestry. Put another way, "While Satan has sought to destroy the living tree, trying to uproot it, he has only been like a gardener digging with his spade and loosening the earth to help the roots to spread themselves. And when he has been with his ax seeking to lop the Lord's trees and mar their beauty, what has he been, after all, but a pruning knife in the hand of God to take away the branches that do not bear fruit and purge those that do bear some that they might bring forth more fruit." [5]

SEVEN

The Covering of Salvation

Take the helmet of salvation. (Ephesians 6:17)

I will never forget the day I first saw her. I arrived home after a taxing day at the office, walked through the front door, and shouted, "Kathy, I'm home!" No response. I looked in all the usual places—the kitchen, the laundry room, the bedroom—but Kathy was nowhere to be found. Suddenly, I became aware of a soft sobbing sound. "Is that you, Kathy?" I asked as I moved toward the sound—still no answer. As I walked into the bathroom, I saw my wife looking down at a tiny form in the palm of her hand. Sensing my presence, she looked up resolutely and said, "Her name is Grace."

As I looked down at my ninth child, Kathy began to share a vision she experienced earlier that afternoon. Six weeks pregnant, she had returned home deeply troubled after a routine doctor's visit. Her obstetrician had expressed concern regarding the viability of our preborn child. So Kathy went straight to bed and began to pray. "Show me your will, Lord," she pleaded. "You know how desperately I want another baby." In the ensuing hours she asked God to show her his grace.

After a protracted period of intensive prayer, Kathy saw an image. A little girl was walking away from her, hand in hand with the Lord. The girl bounced along in perfect peace and harmony. Suddenly she turned and looked directly into Kathy's eyes. "Good-bye, Mommy," she said. Instinctively Kathy blurted out, "I just want to hug you." At that very moment she felt an intense presence—and then she began to bleed.

When I encountered Kathy standing in the bathroom, she was cradling a perfectly formed embryo in her hands. "Why Grace?" I asked, curious about the name Kathy had chosen. Without a moment's hesitation she responded, "God has answered my prayers and has given me his grace. He has shown me that I didn't lose our baby. I know exactly where she is."

That day I gained a fresh perspective on the helmet of salva-tion. In the midst of the deepest pain a mother can experi-ence, the helmet of

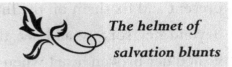

The helmet of salvation blunts the blow of death and enables us to view our circumstances from the perspective of eternity.

salvation had served to protect my wife's perspective. As the breastplate of righteousness is a spiritual heart protec-tor, the helmet of salvation is a spiritual head protector. It is the covering that protects our minds so that we do not become disoriented in the throes of spiritual warfare. When the denizens of darkness land their most devastat-ing blows, the helmet of salvation guards our minds and grants us perspective.

First and foremost, the helmet of salvation blunts the blow of death and enables us to view our circumstances from the perspective of eternity. For Kathy, the death of our baby was the ultimate disorienting blow, yet a glimpse of the salvation that is to come blunted its edge. The helmet of salvation allowed her to take her eyes off the present and fix them on the future. It enabled her to look beyond her sorrow and see the promise of salvation. It healed her broken heart when nothing else would do.

Postmodernity seeks to deny death by driving it into the closet, to trivialize it by treating it irreverently, or to circumvent it through the use of clichés. In sharp distinction, Christianity demonstrates that death is defeated. Cultural thanatologists may urge us to accept death as a friend, but Christian theology sees death as the enemy. Says Philip Yancey, "Christian faith does not offer us a peaceful way to come to terms with death. No, it offers instead a way to overcome death. Christ stands for Life, and his resurrection should give convincing proof that God is not satisfied with any 'cycle of life' that ends in death. He will go to any extent—he *did* go to any extent—to break that cycle."[1]

This is the message that radiates from the lips of righteous Job. Satan had wielded the sword of death with devastating fury. He butchered Job's livestock. He murdered Job's legacy. And if God had permitted him to do so, he would have snuffed out Job's life. The devil's devastation was so complete that Job's wife had lost all perspective. With her mind careening out of control, she cried, "Curse God and die!" (Job 2:9). Job, however, saw his plight from the perspective of eternity. Having donned the helmet of salvation, he was empowered to declare, "I know that my Redeemer lives, and that in the end he will stand upon the earth. And after my skin has been destroyed, yet in my flesh I will see God; I myself will see him with my own eyes—I, and not another. How my heart yearns within me!" (Job 19:25–27).

Furthermore, the helmet of salvation blunts the disorienting blow of doubt. When Kathy's obstetrician expressed concern regarding the viability of our baby, Kathy experienced a mind-numbing sense of foreboding. Ferocious waves of fear swept away all perspective. She was plagued by the possibility that she would never see her baby alive. Yet in the center of the storm she regained her perspective. The promise of salvation assuaged her doubts and drove away her dread. God gave her a glimpse of glory. And she was filled with the certainty that one day soon she would see her baby again—only this time in a glorious resurrected body perfectly engineered for a renewed universe. As she expressed it on the day of baby Grace's funeral: "If you lose something, you don't know where it is. I *know* where my baby is. And I *know* whom she is with."

That ultimately was the perspective of Job. The certainty of salvation not only assured him that in his flesh he would see God, but it assured him that in his flesh he would once again see his children. As Yancey aptly puts it: "The author takes pains to point out that in the end Job received double all he had lost in his time of trials: 14,000 sheep to replace the 7,000; 6,000 camels to replace 3,000; a thousand oxen and donkeys to replace 500. There is one exception: previously Job had seven sons and three daughters, and in the restoration he got back seven sons and three daughters—the same number, not double."

Yancey goes on to suggest that the divine author might well have been hinting at heaven. "From that view Job did indeed receive double, ten new children here to go with the ten he would one day rejoin."[2] Often when I am asked how many children I have, I say, "Eight. Four boys and four girls." My kids inevitably correct me. "No, Dad," they say. "We have nine children. Four boys and five girls." In their minds there is no doubt that they have a sister who preceded them to heaven. Life after life is not a crutch or a cop-out; it is a certainty. As Christians, we stake our lives on the hope that God "will transform our lowly bodies so that they will be like his glorious body" (Philippians 3:21).

Finally, the helmet of salvation serves to blunt the devastating blow of disappointment. I do not pretend to comprehend or even to be able to fully relate to the disappointment a woman experiences when a baby dies—although over the last year I have gotten a glimpse of the toll it has taken on my wife. Disappointments, however, do not merely manifest in the dramatic. Disappointments accumulate over time, burying hope under an avalanche of despair.

A mother contracts Parkinson's; a father-in-law comes down with cancer; a wife lives with constant pain. Why? Why me? Why doesn't God answer our prayers? Why doesn't he just tell us why? All of these and a host of other questions pulsated through Job's mind in the dead of night. Yet the Book of Job never answers the question why.

Instead, after thirty-plus chapters of men's rambling speculation, God appears and asks some questions of his own: "Who is this that darkens my counsel with words without knowledge? Brace yourself like a man; I will question you, and you shall answer me" (Job 38:2–3). As Frederick Buechner puts it, "God doesn't explain. He explodes. He asks Job who he thinks he is anyway. He says that to try to explain the kind of things Job wants explained would be like trying to explain Einstein to a little-neck clam."[3]

In essence, God asks Job if he would like to try his hand at running the universe for a while. Try creating a lightning bolt. How about producing just a tiny drop of dew? Says Yancey, "The message behind the splendid poetry boils down to this: *Until you know a little more about running the physical universe, Job, don't tell me how to run the moral universe.* . . . The impact of God's speech on Job is almost as amazing as the speech itself. Although God never answers one question about Job's predicament, the blast from the storm flattens Job. He repents in dust and ashes, and every trace of disappointment with God is swept away."[4]

The solution to our disappointments is never found in answering the question why—it is found in trusting God in the midst of our whys. One glimpse of glory and all Kathy's whys faded to black. The helmet of salvation

> *The solution to our disappointments is never found in answering the question why—it is found in trusting God in the midst of our whys.*

permitted her to stand firm against all the devil's schemes and enabled her to look beyond death, doubt, and disappointments toward our destiny. In Kathy's vision, baby Grace walked away in perfect peace and harmony, hand in hand with her Lord. When Kathy next sees her, Grace will be walking into her embrace.

EIGHT

The Covering of Scripture

Take . . . the sword of the Spirit, which is the word of God.
(Ephesians 6:17)

It was the ultimate spiritual battle. The Creator was alone and hungry, and the most powerful creature in the universe was poised and ready to strike. Jesus had fasted forty days and forty nights. Sensing vulnerability, the tempter seized the moment. "If you are the Son of God, tell these stones to become bread," he hissed (Matthew 4:3). Jesus might well have responded by unveiling his divine glory, but he didn't. He took up "the sword of the Spirit, which is the word of God" (Ephesians 6:17).

Next, Satan transported Jesus to the pinnacle of the temple. " 'If you are the Son of God,' he said, 'throw your-self down.' For it is written: 'He will command his angels concerning you, and they will lift you up in their hands, so that you will not strike your foot against a stone' "

(Matthew 4:6). Jesus could have routed Satan with twelve legions of angels, but he didn't. He took up the sword of the Spirit.

In desperation, the devil took the Lord to the summit of a high mountain and showed him the kingdoms of the world and their splendor. "'All this I will give you,' he said, 'if you will bow down and worship me'" (Matthew 4:9). The Lord of the universe could have blinded the devil with the brilliance of his intellect, but he didn't. He took up the sword of the Spirit.

As Jesus armed himself with "the sword of the Spirit, which is the word of God," so must we. Armed with the puny sword of reason, we stand impotent before an arch-fiend who has studied us thoroughly and is intimately acquainted with all of our vulnerabilities. Armed with the sword of the Spirit, however, we are a terror to Satan and can stand strong in the face of his fiercest temptations. As William Gurnall has well said, "Throughout the ages the sword has been a most necessary part of the soldier's equipment and has been used more than any other weapon. A pilot without his chart, a student without his book, a soldier without his sword—all are ridiculous. But above these, it is absurd to think of being a Christian without knowledge of God's Word and some skill to use this weapon."[1]

> *It is not enough to have the Word of God in our homes or in our hands. We must deftly wield it on the battlefield of life.*

We must ever be mindful that the Word of God was not forged by human hands, but by the Spirit. He alone gives the sword its edge. And he alone can teach us how to rightly use it. It was the Spirit who instructed Paul to write, "*take* the sword" (Ephesians 6:17; emphasis added). Thus, we are reminded that it is not enough to have the Word of God in our homes or in our hands. We must deftly wield it on the battlefield of life.

This means that we are equipped to mine the treasure that is buried in the Word. Says Spurgeon, "Let it never be said that God has recorded truths in His word that you have not read. Study the word and work out its meaning. Go deep into the spirit of inspiration. He gets the most gold who digs the deepest in this mine. The deeper you go under the Spirit's guidance, the larger the reward for your toil."[2]

MINING SCRIPTURE

To assist us in the task of mining Scripture, it is helpful to employ the acronym LIGHTS.[3] For just as helmet lights assist miners in discovering gold beneath the surface of the earth, so the acronym LIGHTS will aid you in discerning buried treasure within the pages of Scripture. The "L" in LIGHTS will serve to remind us of the *literal principle* of biblical interpretation. In simple terms, this means that we are to interpret the Word of God just as we interpret other forms of communication—in its most obvious and literal sense. When Scripture uses a metaphor or a figure of speech, we should interpret it accordingly. Thus, when Jesus says he is "the door," it should be readily apparent that he is not composed of wood and hinges; rather, he is the "way" into salvation.

No single principle is more misused by modern-day deliverance advocates than this. Bob Larson, for example, abuses this principle in order to read esoteric meanings into biblical passages. According to Larson, "literalizing" Scripture means to wield the "Bible as though it were an actual weapon, dealing lethal paper cuts to demons, even making eunuchs out of incubi. Other creative uses of Scripture include restraining demons with invisible rope (because 'a cord of three strands is not quickly broken') and raising a person's body temperature by holding a Bible over the individual (because the Word of God is like a lamp)."[4]

The "I" in LIGHTS reminds us of the *illumination* principle. Though the Word of God is the sword of the Spirit, when we grasp it, his illuminating power floods our being. Says Paul, "We have not received the spirit of the world but the Spirit who is from God, that we may understand what God has freely given us" (1 Corinthians 2:12). The Spirit of truth not only provides insights that permeate the mind, but also provides illumination that penetrates the heart.

Clearly, however, the Holy Spirit does not supplant the scrupulous study of Scripture. Rather, He provides us with insights that can only be spiritually discerned. In this way the Holy Spirit helps us to *exegete* (draw out of) rather than *eisegete* (read into) Scripture. He only illumines what is *in* the text; illumination does *not* go *beyond* the text.

As with the literal principle, advocates of deliverance prostitute the *illumination* principle. As a case in point, Neil Anderson abuses 1 Corinthians 4:5 to support the theory that children's traumatic memories may be repressed as an act of God's mercy until a spiritual support network is in place. He specifically misuses the phrase "he will bring to light what is hidden in darkness" to assure people that what they "remember" after they ask God to reveal "what is hidden in darkness" is indeed true. Obviously, this verse has nothing to do with repressed memories! Rather, it is a clear reference to the time when we will stand in God's presence while he reveals the motives of our hearts.

The "G" in LIGHTS is reminiscent of the word *grammar*. Scripture must always be interpreted in accordance with typical rules of grammar, including syntax, style, and semantics. For this reason, it is important that the student of Scripture have a basic understanding of the grammatical principles. It is also helpful to have a grasp of the original biblical languages. If you do not know Greek or Hebrew, however, don't panic. Today there are a host of eminently usable tools to aid you in gaining insights from the original biblical languages. Such tools, along with some common sense, will keep you from being fooled by people who claim a mastery of the biblical languages while undermining the art and science of biblical interpretation.

In fact, even those who do command a mastery over the original languages are not immune to error in this regard. Dr. Clinton Arnold, for example, interprets Paul's use of the Greek word *topos* in Ephesians 4:27—"do not give the devil a *foothold*"—as spatial language, suggesting that a Christian can be demon-possessed. Common sense, however, precludes his interpretation. As demonstrated by the immediate context, Paul is simply warning believers against giving the devil a chance or opportunity.[5] Further, as previously demonstrated, the whole of Scripture precludes the contention that Christians can be demon-possessed.

The "H" in LIGHTS reminds us that the Christian faith

is *historical* (see Luke 1 : 1–4). Thus, the biblical text is best understood when one is familiar with the customs, culture, and historical context of biblical times. Such background information is extremely helpful in drawing out the full meaning of any given text. It's crucial, however, not to read more into the historical context than what is warranted.

For example, as a historian, Arnold is well aware of the fact that Ephesus was rife with occultism. Unfortunately, he draws the unwarranted conclusion that Christians must have continued to involve themselves in magical practices— even going so far as making "specific invitations to gods, goddesses, and assistant spirits to come, take residence, and manifest their presence in a variety of ways."[6] Therefore, he concludes that Paul must have been delivering Christians of their demons. While it is helpful to understand the historical context, such leaps of logic are clearly not warranted.

The "T" in LIGHTS serves to remind us that even though ultimate illumination of Scripture comes from the Holy Spirit, God has also provided the church with uniquely gifted human *teachers* (see Ephesians 4:11). There is, however, a wide chasm between those who are skilled in the art and science of biblical interpretation and those who read their own peculiar preferences into the text. James no doubt had this distinction in mind when he solemnly warned, "Not many of you should presume to be teachers, my brothers, because you know that we who teach will be judged more strictly" (James 3:1). Paul echoed the same warning when he exhorted Timothy, "Do your best to present yourself to God as one approved, a workman who does not need to be ashamed and who correctly handles the word of truth" (2 Timothy 2:15).

Scripture makes it abundantly clear that the task of teaching should never be taken lightly. Following the example of the Bereans (see Acts 17:11), we must make sure that what human teachers teach is in line with what Scripture has already taught (see 1 Thessalonians 5:21). Put another way, all of us must be so familiar with truth that when counterfeits appear on the horizon we can identify them instantaneously.

Finally, the "S" in LIGHTS reminds us of the principle of *scriptural harmony*. Simply stated, this means that individual passages of Scripture must always harmonize with Scripture as a whole. One text can never be interpreted in such a way as to conflict with other passages. If a particular passage can be interpreted in several ways, the only choice is the interpretation that harmonizes with the rest of Scripture. The biblical interpreter must keep in mind that all of Scripture, though communicated through various human instruments, has one single Author. And that Author does not contradict himself.

In the ultimate spiritual battle, the deceiver quoted an Old Testament passage and contextualized it with a seductive suggestion. Jesus, however, immediately restored order by harmonizing Satan's pretext with the rest of Scripture. As followers of Christ, we must be prepared to emulate his example.

MEMORIZING SCRIPTURE

Wielding the sword of the Spirit, which is the Word of God, involves not only *mining Scripture*, but also *memorizing*

Scripture. As Charles Swindoll points out, no single spiritual discipline is more prudent or practical than Scripture memorization: "No other single discipline is more useful and rewarding than this. No other single exercise pays greater spiritual dividends! Your *prayer life* will be strengthened. Your *witnessing* will be sharper and much more effective. Your *counseling* will be in demand. Your *attitudes* and *outlook* will begin to change. Your

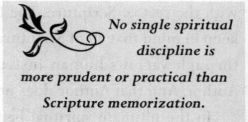

No single spiritual discipline is more prudent or practical than Scripture memorization.

mind will become alert and observant. Your *confidence* and *assurance* will be enhanced. Your *faith* will be solidified."[7]

Despite such marvelous benefits, far too few Christians have made Scripture memorization a lifestyle. For the most part, it is not because they don't *want* to, but because they have never been taught *how* to. Thus they suppose that they have bad memories, when in reality they simply have *untrained* memories. Having taught memory for decades, I am convinced that anyone, regardless of age or acumen, can ably memorize Scripture. God has called us to write his Word on the tablets of our hearts (see Proverbs 7:1–3; cf. Deuteronomy 6:6), and with the call he has provided the ability commensurate with the task (see 2 Corinthians 9:8; Philippians 4:13). Your mind is like a muscle. If you exercise it, you will increase its capacity to recall information. If you don't, like a muscle, it will atrophy. Here are some practical tips to get started:

- *Set goals.* He who aims at nothing invariably hits it.
- *Make your goals attainable.* If your goals are unrealistic, you will undoubtedly become discouraged and give up.
- *Memorize with a family member or friend.* Memorizing with someone else is not only enjoyable, but will also make you accountable.
- *Use normally unproductive time to review what you have memorized.* Opportunities for review include waiting in lines, falling asleep, etc.

And remember, there's no time like the present to get started! A good place to begin is Psalm 119. In fact, committing verse 11 of that passage to memory—"I have hidden your word in my heart that I might not sin against you"—may well encourage you to make Scripture memorization a lifestyle.

MEDITATING ON SCRIPTURE

Finally, to take the sword of the Spirit, which is the Word of God, involves *meditating on Scripture*. In our day, pagan religions such as Buddhism have virtually cornered the meditation market. Phil Jackson, coach of the Los Angeles Lakers (a.k.a. the Zen Master) even used Buddhist meditation to get his team ready for the NBA's Western Conference Finals. Pagan meditation, however, should not preclude proper meditation.

Buddhist meditation seeks to stamp out the self—to become one with the impersonal cosmic consciousness of the universe. In sharp distinction, biblical meditation seeks to center one's self on the personal Creator of the universe. And it does so through a singular focus on Scripture. To meditate on a passage is to memorize it, to process it, to think deeply about it, and then to offer it back to God as we pray "in the Spirit on all occasions." Says J. I. Packer, "In meditation, the whole man is engaged in deep and prayerful thought on the true meaning and bearing of a particular passage."[8]

It is not accidental that Jesus often withdrew to lonely places for prayer and meditation. As Jesus longed to be alone with his heavenly Father, so must we. As I noted in *The Prayer of Jesus,* the issue is not location but motivation. We are all unique creations of God; thus, your secret place will no doubt be different than mine. But we all desperately need a place away from the invasive sounds of this world so that we can hear the sounds of another place and another voice.

In the ultimate spiritual battle, Jesus took up the sword of the Spirit, which is the Word of God. He had mined, memorized, and meditated on Scripture. Thus, when the slanderer sought to tempt the Savior to turn stones into bread, Jesus was prepared. "It is written," he said, "Man does not live on bread alone, but on every word that comes from the mouth of God" (Matthew 4:4).

NINE

The Covering of Prayer

> *Pray in the Spirit on all occasions*
> *with all kinds of prayers and requests.*
> *With this in mind, be alert and always keep on*
> *praying for all the saints.* (Ephesians 6:18)

It would be hard for me to fully describe the spiritual conflict I experienced as I wrote *The Covering*. At times I had an irrational certainty that I would not—could not—finish the project. It was as though I could smell the tempter's putrid breath as I was bombarded with the disorienting blows of doubt, discouragement, and despair. While I could not discern his seditious slurs with my physical ears, somehow they penetrated "the ear" of my mind.

It was in the throes of spiritual battle—when I was certain I could no longer stand—that I inevitably crumpled into a position of power. For on my knees in my secret place, I was once again emboldened to stand firm "against the spiritual forces of evil in the heavenly realms" (Ephesians 6:12).

The Covering of Prayer

PRAY IN THE SPIRIT ON ALL OCCASIONS

Prayer is not a mere piece of the covering; it is much more than that. Prayer is indelibly woven into each piece of the covering. It is to the armor what oxygen is to the lungs. Prayer is the given, the foundation, the first principle of spiritual warfare. Little wonder then that the apostle Paul urges us to "pray in the Spirit on all occasions" (Ephesians 6:18). To do so is to pray in concert with the will and purposes of God. Only as the Spirit empowers our prayers in accordance with God's will is the covering finally complete.

This is the essence of ending our prayers with the word *amen*. It is far more significant than simply signing off or saying, "That's all." With "amen" we are in effect saying, "May it be so in accordance with the will of God." It is a marvelous reminder that any discussion on prayer must begin with the understanding that prayer is a means of bringing us into conformity with God's will, not a magic mantra that ensures God's conformity to ours.

To "pray in the Spirit on all occasions," then, is to

recognize the sovereignty of God over every detail of our lives. In effect it is a way of saying, "Thank God this world is under his control, not mine!" In the yielded life there is great peace in knowing that God has every detail of our lives under control. He will not spare us from trials and temptations but will use the fiery furnace to purge impurities from our lives.

Furthermore, to "pray in the Spirit on all occasions" is to take up the sword of *the Spirit,* which is the Word of God. One of the most amazing aspects of the sword is that it is alive and active, not dead and dull. Indeed, God still speaks today through the mystery of his Word. Thus with Samuel, we can say, "Speak, [Lord,] for your servant is listening" (1 Samuel 3:10).

As we listen, we must also "test the spirits." Says John, "Do not believe every spirit, but test the spirits to see whether they are from God, because many false prophets have gone out into the world" (1 John 4:1). Satan's foremost strategy of seduction is to disguise himself as an angel of enlightenment (see 2 Corinthians 11:14). His slickest slogan is "Feel, don't think."

God's Spirit, on the other hand, illumines our minds so that we may understand what he has freely given us (see 1 Corinthians 2:12). Before becoming Christians, reading the Bible was like reading someone else's mail. Now, however, the Scriptures have become sixty-six love letters from God, addressed specifically to us. As Jesus so beautifully expressed, "My sheep listen to my voice; I know them, and they follow me" (John 10:27).

Finally, to "pray in the Spirit on all occasions" means to continually meditate on Scripture. Ultimately, our prayers are only as inspired as our intake of Scripture. It's better to read a single passage and meditate on it, than to read an entire book of the Bible and not think deeply about it. Scripture feeds meditation, and meditation gives food to our prayers. As Puritan writer William Bridge put it, "Reading without meditation is unfruitful; meditation without reading is hurtful; to meditate and to read without prayer upon both, is without blessing."[1]

Donald Whitney, who rightly refers to meditation as "the missing link between Bible intake and prayer," notes that if there was a "secret" to George Müller's prayer life, it was his discovery of the connection between meditation and prayer. Müller discovered that after meditating on Scripture he was enabled to more naturally transition into a marvelous time of meaningful prayer.

WITH ALL KINDS OF PRAYERS AND REQUESTS

As George Müller discovered, we can rightly bring God our requests only within the context of a relationship that is nourished by meditation. As I noted in *The Prayer of Jesus,* most of us do precisely the inverse. We rush into God's presence with a laundry list of prayer requests. And before our knees have ever touched the ground, we are already thinking about getting back into our frenzied lifestyles. Often we treat our heavenly Father no better than we treat our families. We want a relationship without the discipline of investing quality time.

Thus, before Jesus teaches his disciples how to bring God their requests, he first teaches them how to build a relationship. Prayer begins with a humble faith in the love and resources of our heavenly Father. Such faith inevitably leads to adoration as we express our longing for an ever deeper and richer relationship with the one who knit us together in our mothers' wombs. The more we get to know him, the more we are inclined to confess our unworthiness and to thank him for his grace. It is only in the context of such a relationship that we can rightly bring God our requests. Says R. C. Sproul, "Only after God has been rightly honored, adored, and exalted, do the subsequent petitions of God's people assume their proper place."[2]

The prayer of Jesus, often called the "Lord's Prayer," is neatly divided into two parts. The first is focused on God's glory. Thus, we pray, "hallowed be your name, your kingdom come, your will be done." The second is focused on our requests. In the words of the great church father Tertullian: "How gracefully has the Divine Wisdom arranged the order of the prayer; so that *after* things heavenly—that is, after the 'Name' of God, the 'Will' of God, and the 'Kingdom' of God—it should give earthly necessities also room for a petition!"[3]

To pray in the Spirit on all occasions "with all kinds of

prayers and requests" first entails petitioning our heavenly Father for daily provisions. Thus Jesus taught his disciples to pray, "Give us today our daily bread." As the Holy Spirit is an all-encompassing gift, so too we are reminded that "bread" encompasses far more than food. In the words of sixteenth-century theologian Martin Chemnitz, "The word 'bread' in this petition encompasses all things belonging to and necessary for the sustenance of this body and life."[4]

Furthermore, to pray in the Spirit on all occasions "with all kinds of prayers and requests" encompasses daily petitioning our heavenly Father for pardon. When we pray, "Forgive us our debts, as we also have forgiven our debtors," we are reminded of the infinite price that was paid so that we might be forgiven. We must ever be mindful that it was God himself who hung on the cross so that we could be reconciled to him for time and for eternity.

Finally, to pray in the Spirit on all occasions "with all kinds of prayers and requests" involves praying for protection. Thus Jesus concluded the model prayer by teaching his disciples to pray, "And lead us not into temptation, but deliver us from the evil one." In doing so we are reminded that God is in control of all things, including the temptations of Satan. As Martin Luther has well said, the devil is "God's devil." Even in the ultimate temptation Jesus was "led *by the Spirit* in the desert, where for forty days he was tempted by the devil" (Luke 4:1; emphasis added). Satan was the *agent* of the temptation. God, however, was the *author* of the testing. Satan used the occasion to tempt Christ to sin; God used the occasion to demonstrate that he could not sin!

BE ALERT AND ALWAYS KEEP ON PRAYING FOR ALL THE SAINTS

The word *alert* took on new meaning after the terrorist attacks of September 11, 2001. While America slumbered, the forces of terrorism sent flaming missiles deep into her soul. That is precisely how the ultimate terrorist works. He loves to lull us to sleep and then to strike with devastating fury. He is pleased when we suppose he is everywhere—or imagine he is nowhere at all; when we think he can control

We do not pray as lone soldiers, but as an army standing united against a common foe.

us against our wills— or envision he cannot influence us at all. He is the quintessential master of disguises.

"With this in mind," says Paul, "be *alert* and always keep on praying for all the saints" (Ephesians 6:18; emphasis added). His words hearken back to the admonition of the Master, who warned the slumbering disciples, "Watch and pray so that you will not fall into temptation" (Matthew 26:41). Peter extends the warning by urging us, "Be self-controlled and alert. Your enemy the devil prowls around like a roaring lion looking for someone to devour. Resist him, standing firm in the faith" (1 Peter 5:8–9). Only as you watch and pray can you "take your stand against the devil's schemes" (Ephesians 6:11).

Furthermore, we are to "keep on praying for *all* the saints." Put another way, we are to pray in plural. We do not pray as lone soldiers, but as an army standing united against a common foe. Thus we pray not only for our own needs, but for the needs of our extended family as well. When terrorism struck the heart of America, we stood as one against a common foe. Likewise, when the ultimate terrorist comes "to steal and kill and destroy" (John 10:10), we are called to pray not as rugged individualists, but as members of a community of faith.

Finally, it is not by accident that Paul refers to fellow believers as "saints." He calls us saints not because we are pure, but because we are called to purity. The instant we prayed to receive the righteousness of Christ as our covering, the process of becoming pure was initiated and the promise of its completion sure. In the meantime, we look forward with rapt anticipation to the day when we will be completely set free from all temptations. The tempter will be thrown into the lake of burning sulfur (see Revelation 20:10), and temptations will be no more. We will enter the golden city with divine assurance that "nothing impure will ever enter it, nor will anyone who does what is shameful or deceitful, but only those whose names are written in the Lamb's book of life" (Revelation 21:27).

TEN

The Covering as a Lifestyle

Therefore everyone who hears these words of mine
and puts them into practice is like a wise man. (Matthew 7:24)

My objective in The Prayer of Jesus was to effect a major paradigm shift in our perceptions about prayer—a shift from seeing prayer as merely a means of bringing our requests to seeing prayer as an opportunity to build a relationship with the Lover of our souls. Likewise, *The Covering* is designed to effect a major paradigm shift in our perceptions about spiritual warfare. The key to supernatural protection in the invisible war is not found in *exorcising* demons, but in *exercising* spiritual disciplines. Ultimately, only as we "put on the full armor of God" can we take our "stand against the devil's schemes" (Ephesians 6:11).

To put on the covering as a lifestyle assumes not only that you understand what the full armor of God represents, but that you are able to remember each piece of the armor as well. All of memory can be reduced to the process of making associations——a name with a face, a state with a capital, or a chapter in the Bible with its content. If the pieces of information are correctly associated, when you think of one, the other will immediately pop into your mind as well.

The following associations should help you recall the individual pieces of armor:

Truth——As you put on your belt each morning, imagine that the buckle is fashioned out of a gigantic tooth. (The more unusual the association, the easier it is to remember!) As your waist is the center of your body, so

PICTURE THIS!

The best way to remember information is to see it joined together or associated in a mental picture. It has been accurately said that one best remembers what is first visualized. As you learn to make conscious associations through the use of mental pictures, you will soon discover that you can recall information quickly and easily. Once the information is firmly rooted in your mind, the visual associations are no longer necessary.

truth is central to the full armor of God. Without it, the covering that protects you from the devil's schemes simply crumples to the ground, leaving you naked and vulnerable.

Righteousness—As you button your shirt or blouse, picture yourself putting on the breastplate of righteousness. (You might even imagine a rye-cheese mess all over your shirt or blouse.) And remember, no matter how correct your worldview, if it is not coupled with righteousness, you inevitably forfeit the moral authority to speak.

Peace—As you put on your shoes each day, remember that the priceless material with which God has fitted your feet for readiness in spiritual warfare is nothing less than the gospel of peace. (Imagine peas in your shoes to remind you of peace—remember, the more outrageous the association, the easier it is to recall.) With your feet fashioned with the readiness that comes from the gospel of peace, you can stand firm in distress, disease, destruction, and even death.

Faith—Each time you look at the face in the mirror, picture taking up the shield of faith (face). As the ancient shield enveloped the body, so faith envelops your entire being. When Satan attacks your head, the hand of faith holds fast to truth. When Satan attacks your heart, the hand of faith holds fast to righteousness. In fact, it might well be said that the shield of faith is the apex of your armor. It is the grace "with which you can extinguish *all* the flaming arrows of the evil one."

Salvation——Every time you comb your hair, associate that simple action with putting on the helmet of salvation. Just as the breastplate of righteousness is your spiritual heart protector, the helmet of salvation is your spiritual head protector. It is the covering that protects your mind so that you do not become disoriented in the throes of spiritual warfare. When the denizens of darkness land their most devastating blows, the helmet of salvation will guard your mind and grant you perspective.

Scripture——From this day forward, as you pick up your Bible, may "the sword of the Spirit, which is the Word of God," flash through your mind. Armed with the puny sword of reason, you stand impotent before an archfiend who has studied you thoroughly and is intimately acquainted with all your vulnerabilities. Armed with the sword of the Spirit, however, you are a terror to Satan and can stand strong in the face of his fiercest temptations.

Prayer—Finally, each time you open your eyes in the morning or close them at the end of the day, remember that prayer is firing the winning shot. Prayer is not merely a piece of the armor; rather, it is the thread that weaves the covering into an exquisite tapestry. It is the given, the foundation, the first principle of God's plan to protect you from evil!

It is my prayer that you will experience God's supernatural protection in the invisible war as you put on the covering as a lifestyle. And that in the end you with Paul can say, "I have fought the good fight, I have finished the race, I have kept the faith. Now there is in store for me the crown of righteousness, which the Lord, the righteous judge, will award to me on that day—and not only to me, but to all who have longed for his appearing" (2 Timothy 4:7–8).

NOTES

Introduction

1. Clinton E. Arnold, *3 Crucial Questions about Spiritual Warfare* (Grand Rapids, Mich.: Baker, 1997), 28.

2. Malcolm McGrath, *Demons of the Modern World* (Amherst, N.Y.: Prometheus Books, 2002), 118-19. See also Bill Ellis, *Raising the Devil: Satanism, New Religions, and the Media* (Lexington, Ky.: The University Press of Kentucky, 2000), 33–34.

3. McGrath, *Demons of the Modern World*, 119–21; 226–30; Ellis, *Raising the Devil*, 34–35.

4. McGrath, *Demons of the Modern World*, 103.

5. Ibid., 106–18.

6. Michael W. Cuneo, *American Exorcism* (New York: Doubleday, 2001), xiii. As sociologist Jeffrey Victor notes, whether one's "demons" are Satanists or Communists, witches or governments, they all become generalized scapegoats for the social ills of their respective societies (Jeffrey S. Victor, *Satanic Panic: The Creation of a Contemporary Legend* [Chicago: Open Court Press, 1993], 195–205).

7. I am indebted to the progression of thought provided by Michael Cuneo in *American Exorcism* from "The Blatty Factor" to "The Rise of Deliverance Ministry," 3–58.

8. Cuneo, *American Exorcism*, 17.

9. Ibid., 29.

10. Ibid., 30.

11. Ibid., 31-32.

12. Ibid., 43.

13. Ibid., 45.

14. Ibid., 43, 47.

15. Ibid., 46.

16. Cuneo, *American Exorcism*, 51. Peck was only one of the authorities respected by the secular world who embraced demonology explanation for human woes. As

author Malcolm McGrath notes, "The scare was promoted by medical doctors, psychology Ph.D.s, district attorneys, and a host of law-enforcement officials" (McGrath, *Demons of the Modern World,* 249).

17. Bob Larson, *Larson's Book of Spiritual Warfare* (Nashville: Thomas Nelson, 1999), 6.

18. Bob Larson, "The Devil: Who He Is and What He Does" (Denver: Bob Larson Ministries, 1996), side 2, audiotape.

19. Larson, *In the Name of Satan* (Nashville: Thomas Nelson, 1996), 160.

20. Larson, *Larson's Book of Spiritual Warfare,* 1–2, 6.

21. Larson, *In the Name of Satan,* 151.

22. Elliot Miller, "The Bondage Maker: Examining the Message and Method of Neil T. Anderson," Part One, *Christian Research Journal* 22, no. 1 (Summer 1998): 18; see also Part Three in this series; both articles available on-line at www.equip.org. See Neil T. Anderson, *Helping Others Find Freedom in Christ* (Ventura, Calif.: Regal, 1995), 144–45, 279.

23. Neil Anderson, *Spiritual Conflict and Biblical Counseling* (n.d.), videotape on file at Christian Research Institute.

24. Neil T. Anderson, *The Bondage Breaker* (Eugene, Ore.: Harvest House, 1990), 101.

25. Ibid., 85–86.

26. Ibid., 102.

27. Ibid., 202.

28. See Dr. Neil Anderson, *Released from Bondage* (Nashville: Thomas Nelson, 1993), 69; and Anderson, *Helping Others Find Freedom in Christ,* 49.

29. See Anderson, *Helping Others Find Freedom in Christ,* 296–97.

30. See Anderson, *The Bondage Breaker,* 107.

31. Bob Larson, "How to Call Up a Demon" (Denver: Bob Larson Ministries, 1999), side 2, audiotape.

32. For example, Lutheran pastoral counselor Kurt Koch, Dallas Theological Seminary professor of theology Merrill Unger, Wheaton College president V. Raymond Edman, *Christian Life* editor Russell Meade, among others (see Ellis, *Raising the Devil,* 46–47).

Notes

33. Cuneo, *American Exorcism,* 92. Cf. Don Basham, *Deliver Us from Evil* (Grand Rapids: Chosen Books, 1972), 101–106.

34. Basham, *Deliver Us from Evil,* 104–5 (emphasis in original).

35. Prince is not alone. In *Biblical Demonology,* Dr. Unger argued that Christians are not subject to demonic inhabitation because the Holy Spirit indwells them. As Dr. Clinton Arnold notes, however, several decades later Unger changed his perspective "as a result of numerous letters from missionaries all over the world claiming that they had witnessed cases of true believers manifesting possession behavior" (Arnold, *3 Crucial Questions,* 76). Former Wheaton College president Edman even argued that the theological issue was "irrelevant": "Theory says, 'no,' but the facts say, 'yes.' According to standard Christian theology, it is true that a demon could not remain in the body of a Christian who has received the Holy Spirit. However, I know true Christians who were truly demon possessed, and who were delivered in answer to prayer given in the name of the Lord Jesus'" (quoted in Ellis, *Raising the Devil,* 47).

36. I am not questioning the sincerity of those who have had a subjective experience that conflicts with Scripture, only their explanations for such experiences. Deliverance ministers such as Bob Larson use peer pressure, expectations, the subtle power of suggestion, and other sociopsychological manipulation techniques to trap their subjects in a dangerous web of such subjective experiences. It should also be noted that some people are far more suggestible than others. Such fantasy proneness is typically referred to as Grade Five Syndrome. While Grade Five personalities are generally very intuitive and intelligent, they also have vivid visual imaginations. Thus, they are particularly susceptible to the power of suggestion. For further detail on how sociopsychological factors can account for subjective experiences, see my book *Counterfeit Revival* expanded and updated (Nashville: Word, 2001), Part Five.

Chapter One: The Devil Made Me Do It

1. Public debate between Clinton Arnold and Elliot Miller, Evangelical Theological Society Northwest, 3 March 2001, audiotape. Arnold gives

NOTES

another account of the story in *3 Crucial Questions about Spiritual Warfare* (73–74), in which he employs a fictional name (Rin) for Edmund's murderer.

2. Deliverance advocates may respond by arguing that a Christian does not "honor the Father" when he or she sins. Thus, in their view Christians are susceptible to demon possession after all. That, however, is far from true. We honor the Father through faith in Christ, not by virtue of sinless perfectionism. In other words, "honoring the Father" is rooted primarily in our faith, not in our works. We sin because we possess a sin nature, not because we are possessed by devils. In the model prayer, Jesus taught us to pray, "Lead us not into temptation, but deliver us from the evil one" (Matthew 6:13). He did not teach us to pray, "Lead us not into demonization, but deliver us from the evil one." The point should be self-evident. When Christians sin they do so in willful disobedience, not because they are moved against their wills by unseen forces of darkness.

3. C. Fred Dickason, *Demon Possession and the Christian: A New Perspective* (Westchester, Ill.: Crossway, 1987), 124. See also Neil T. Anderson and Robert L. Saucy, *The Common Made Holy* (Eugene, Ore.: Harvest House, 1997), 342; Bob Larson, *Larson's Book of Spiritual Warfare* (Nashville: Thomas Nelson, 1999), 331.

4. *Through It All with Jesus* (Papua New Guinea: SIL Media, n.d.), videotape.

5. Phone conversation with Grace Fabian, 21 February and 18 April 2002.

6. Phone conversation with Roy L. Peterson, 26 February 2002. Subsequent to sharing my primary research with Dr. Arnold (personal meeting, 1 April 2002), he has acknowledged and apologized for factual inaccuracies and errors concerning his account of the murder of Edmund Fabian (see Clinton E. Arnold, "The Christian and Demonic Influence," revised with corrections 6 May 2002, www.westernseminary.edu/papers/Arnold.doc, accessed 11 June 2002).

7. Bob and Gretchen Passantino, *The Spiritual Warfare Movement,* (unpublished manuscript, 1997), 14.

8. Clinton E. Arnold, *3 Crucial Questions about Spiritual Warfare* (Grand Rapids, Mich.: Baker, 1997), 73–74.

9. Jeffrey Burton Russell writes, "The theory of incubi . . . was one of the roots of belief in witchcraft: the witches were supposed to invite such intercourse.

Notes

The idea of incubi does not seem to derive from folk belief, and though the desert fathers told tales of demons taking on the forms of attractive young men and women, incubi do not become significant before the twelfth century. The concept seems to arise from scholastic theory" (*Lucifer: The Devil in the Middle Ages* [Ithaca, N.Y.: Cornell University Press, 1984], 183).

Chapter Two: The Battle for the Mind

1. Charles Spurgeon, compiled and edited by Robert Hall, *Spiritual Warfare in a Believer's Life* (Lynnwood, Wash.: Emerald Books, 1993), 30.
2. C. S. Lewis, *The Screwtape Letters* (New York: Collier Books, 1961), x.
3. Randy Alcorn, *Lord Foulgrin's Letters* (Sisters, Ore.: Multnomah, 2000), 299.

Chapter Three: The Covering of Truth

1. Discussion adapted from Hank Hanegraaff, "Frauds, Fictions, Fantasies, and Fabrications," *Christian Research Journal* 18, no. 3 (Winter 1996): 54.
2. Mike Warnke, with Dave Balsiger and Les Jones, *The Satan Seller* (Plainfield, N.J.: Logos International, 1972), inside front and back cover.
3. Ibid., inside back cover.
4. Ibid., 64.
5. Ibid., 99.
6. See Mike Hertenstein and Jon Trott, *Selling Satan: The Tragic History of Mike Warnke* (Chicago: Cornerstone Press, 1993).
7. Bob and Gretchen Passantino and Jon Trott, "Lauren Stratford: From Satanic Ritual Abuse to Jewish Holocaust Survivor," *Cornerstone Magazine Online,* 13 October 1999, www.cornerstonemag.com/features/iss117/lauren.htm (accessed 8 May 2002); originally published in *Cornerstone,* vol. 28, issue 117 (1999), 12–16, 18.
8. Ibid.
9. Ibid.
10. For details and documentation regarding the falsity of this story see Hank Hanegraaff, *The FACE That Demonstrates the Farce of Evolution,* (Dallas: Word, 1998), 124–25.

NOTES

11. See Proctor & Gamble Web site,www.pg.com/about pg/overview facts/trademark facts.jhtml (accessed 8 May 2002).

12. Still widely circulated through *The Archko Volume,* compiled by W. D. Mahan, which contains all manner of fictional documents purporting the perspective of Jesus' contemporaries, including Joseph and Mary, Herod Antipas, and Caiaphas. For the classic refutation, see Edgar J. Goodspeed, *Modern Apocrypha: Famous "Biblical" Hoaxes* (Boston: The Beacon Press, 1956).

13. See Hank Hanegraaff, "Magic Apologetics," *Christian Research Journal* 20, no. 1 (September/October 1997): 54–55, available on-line at www.equip.org.

14. This story originates in the nineteenth century and has been circulated in various formats by Christian writers such as Bernard Ramm and Henry Morris and in Christian publications such as the *Tyndale Old Testament Commentary, IVP Bible Dictionary,* and *Expositor's Bible Commentary.* According to the story, a whale swallowed a man named James Bartley aboard the *Star of the East.* After the whale was speared and its stomach cut open, Bartley was found somewhat digested but still alive. Not only is there no substantiation for this story, but it does little or nothing to substantiate the biblical account of Jonah and the whale. In the biblical text, God miraculously preserved Jonah's life, and the fish he was swallowed by was specifically prepared by God to do so (see Rich Buhler, "Jonah II: Swallowed Alive!" www.ship-of-fools.com/Myths/index.html, accessed 8 May 2002).

15. This report, circulated worldwide by the Trinity Broadcasting Network (TBN), involves scientists who discovered hell after drilling a hole nine miles into the earth's crust, shoving a microphone into the hole, and hearing the voices of thousands—maybe millions—of tormented souls, screaming in agony. Paul and Jan Crouch, founders of TBN, claimed their tale was documented by major newspaper accounts as well as a letter from a Scandinavian Christian. The documented newspaper account turned out to be nothing more than a fabrication—a sensational story printed by a charismatic Christian tabloid with no factual basis. And the letter turned out to be a hoax concocted by a man named Age Rendalin to demonstrate just how easily Christians can be duped (see Rich Buhler, "Background on the Drilling to Hell story," at www.truthorfiction.com/rumors/drilltohellfacts.htm, accessed 8 May 2002).

120

Notes

16. See Robert C. Newman, "Joshua's Long Day and the NASA Computers: Is the Story True?" at www.reasons.org/resources/apologetics/joshualongday.html, accessed 8 May 2002.

17. For example, The Brownsville Assembly of God (Brownsville, Florida) promoted a video series by David Hogan, in which he claims without evidence his ministry has seen more than two hundred resurrections among remote Mexican Native Americans (*Faith to Raise the Dead,* 4 Parts [Brownsville, Fla.: Brownsville Revival School of Ministry, September 1997]). Benny Hinn claimed, "I was in Ghana just recently when we had half a million people show up, and a man was raised from the dead on the platform. That's a fact, people." When confronted by CNN's John Camp, Hinn replied, "I have not seen it. In that one case, we did hear about it." (Cable News Network: *CNN Impact,* originally aired 16 March 1997); Richard Riss circulates many unsubstantiated resurrection claims, including those of William Branham and Smith Wigglesworth (at www.renewed.net/march97/rriss1.html, accessed 7 June 2002).

18. Os Guinness, *Time for Truth* (Grand Rapids: Baker, 2000), 39.

19. Ibid., 39–40.

20. Adapted from quote attributed to Charles Haddon Spurgeon.

21. As Walter Liefeld puts it, in Isaiah, "the various pieces are part of the armor of God himself, actually aspects of his own character. . . . Righteousness will be his belt and faithfulness the sash around his waist (Isaiah 11:4–5). He put on righteousness as his breastplate, and the helmet of salvation on his head (Isaiah 59:17)" (*Ephesians* [Downers Grove, Ill.: InterVarsity, 1997], 161).

22. Guinness, *Time for Truth,* 79–80.

23. Randy Alcorn, *Lord Foulgrin's Letters* (Sisters, Ore.: Multnomah, 2000), 52.

24. Ibid., 55.

25. Phone conversation with Grace Fabian, 18 April 2002.

Chapter Four: The Covering of Righteousness

1. William Gurnall, *The Christian in Complete Armour,* vol. 2, revised and abridged by Ruthanne Garlock, Kay King, Karen Sloan, and Candy Coan (Edinburgh,

Great Britain: The Banner of Truth Trust, 1988 [originally published in 1658]), 150.

2. For helpful studies of the spiritual disciplines, see Donald S. Whitney, *Spiritual Disciplines for the Christian Life* (Colorado Springs: NavPress, 1991); and Dallas Willard, *The Spirit of the Disciplines* (San Francisco: Harper & Row, 1988).

3. As quoted in Donald S. Whitney, *Spiritual Disciplines for the Christian Life,* 20.

4. Ibid.

5. Dallas Willard, *The Spirit of the Disciplines,* 263.

6. As quoted in *Spurgeon at His Best,* compiled by Tom Carter (Grand Rapids: Baker, 1988), 99–100.

7. C. S. Lewis, *The Screwtape Letters* (New York: Collier, 1961), 11 (emphasis in original).

8. Gurnall, *The Christian in Complete Armour,* vol. 2, 160.

9. Randy Alcorn, *Lord Foulgrin's Letters* (Sisters, Ore.: Multnomah, 2000), 172–174.

Chapter Five: The Covering of Peace

1. Charles Spurgeon, compiled and edited by Robert Hall, *Spiritual Warfare in a Believer's Life* (Lynnwood, Wash.: Emerald Books, 1993), 141.

2. Ibid.

3. Ibid., 145.

4. William Gurnall, *The Christian in Complete Armour,* vol. 2, revised and abridged by Ruthanne Garlock, Kay King, Karen Sloan, and Candy Coan (Edinburgh, Great Britain: The Banner of Truth Trust, 1988 [originally published in 1658]), 333.

Chapter Six: The Covering of Faith

1. William Gurnall, *The Christian in Complete Armour,* vol. 3, revised and abridged by Ruthanne Garlock, Kay King, Karen Sloan, and Candy Coan (Edinburgh, Great Britain: The Banner of Truth Trust, 1989 [originally published in 1662]), 30.

2. Ibid., 31.

3. Discussion partially adapted and modified from Hank Hanegraaff, *Christianity in Crisis* (Eugene, Ore.: Harvest House, 1993), 87, 93, 100, 101. Hebrews 11

is really more about the faithfulness of God than it is about his faithful followers. The opening verses establish that we trust God to fulfill his promises for the future (the unseen) based on what he has already fulfilled in the past. The remainder of the chapter shows how God fulfilled what he had promised to fulfill for those Old Testament saints. Thus, our faith is not blind, but based squarely on God's proven faithfulness.

4. Gurnall, *The Christian in Complete Armour*, vol. 3, 38–39.

5. Spurgeon, *Spiritual Warfare in a Believer's Life*, 38.

Chapter Seven: The Covering of Salvation

1. Philip Yancey, *Where Is God When It Hurts?* (Grand Rapids: Zondervan, 1977), 247. I recommend this book to anyone struggling with pain.

2. Ibid., 253.

3. Quoted in *The Student Bible*, notes by Philip Yancey and Tim Stafford (Grand Rapids: Zondervan, 1986), 489.

4. Philip Yancey, *Disappointment with God* (Grand Rapids: Zondervan, 1988), 190–91. I highly recommend this profound book to anyone struggling with the fairness, silence, or hiddenness of God.

Chapter Eight: The Covering of Scripture

1. William Gurnall, *The Christian in Complete Armour*, vol. 3, revised and abridged by Ruthanne Garlock, Kay King, Karen Sloan, and Candy Coan (Edinburgh, Great Britain: The Banner of Truth Trust, 1989 [originally published in 1662]), 222.

2. Charles Spurgeon, compiled and edited by Robert Hall, *Spiritual Warfare in a Believer's Life* (Lynnwood, Wash.: Emerald Books, 1993), 174.

3. Adapted and modified from Hank Hanegraaff, *Christianity in Crisis* (Eugene, Ore.: Harvest House, 1993), 220–25.

4. Steven Parks, "The Devil Is in the Details: An Examination of the Teachings of Bob Larson," *Christian Research Journal* 24, no. 2 (September/October 1999): 44. "A cord of three strands is not quickly broken" (Ecclesiastes 4:12); "Your word is a lamp to my feet and a light for my path" (Psalms 119:105).

NOTES

5. Arnold's *topos* argument hinges on what he sees as Paul's abundant use of spatial language concerning the Holy Spirit in Ephesians. In context, however, Arnold acknowledges that such "spatial terminology is metaphorical." Furthermore, Arnold acknowledges that the more common interpretation of *topos* here as "chance" or "opportunity" is at least possible. In fact, the New American Standard Bible translates *topos* in Ephesians 4:27 as "opportunity." (As A. T. Robertson points out, "give place to" is idiomatic. For example, Paul says, "Do not take revenge, my friends, but leave room for God's wrath" [Romans 12:19]. See A. T. Robertson, *Word Pictures in the New Testament* [Nashville: Broadman, 1931], 406, 541.) Thus, Ephesians 4:27 does not provide the unambiguous foundation Arnold seeks to show that a demon can inhabit a believer, which foundational proof text he would need since his paradigm is unsupported by the rest of Scripture (see Clinton E. Arnold, *3 Crucial Questions about Spiritual Warfare* [Grand Rapids, Mich.: Baker Books, 1997], 88–89).

6. Arnold, *3 Crucial Questions about Spiritual Warfare,* 92.

7. Charles R. Swindoll, *Seasons of Life* (Sisters, Ore.: Multnomah, 1983), 53 (emphasis in original).

8. John Blanchard, compiler, *More Gathered Gold* (Welwyn, Hertfordshire, England: Evangelical Press, 1986), 202.

Chapter Nine: The Covering of Prayer

1. As quoted in Donald S. Whitney, *Spiritual Disciplines for the Christian Life* (Colorado Springs: NavPress, 1991), 73.

2. R. C. Sproul, *Effective Prayer* (Wheaton, Ill.: Tyndale, 1984), 34.

3. Tertullian, *On Prayer,* VI, in Alexander Roberts and James Donaldson, eds., *The Ante-Nicene Fathers,* vol. III (Grand Rapids: Eerdmans, reprinted in 1986), 683; also quoted in Philip Graham Ryken, *When You Pray* (Wheaton, Ill.: Crossway, 2000), 105.

4. Martin Chemnitz, *The Lord's Prayer* (St. Louis: Concordia, 1999), 57.

CHRISTIAN RESEARCH INSTITUTE

On the Internet
(including 24-Hour Credit Card Ordering):
www.equip.org

By Mail:
CRI United States
P.O. Box 8500
Charlotte, NC 28271-8500

By Phone:
U.S. Toll-Free Customer Service Line (888) 7000-CRI
Fax (704) 887-8299

In Canada:
CRI Canada
56051 Airways P.O.
Calgary, Alberta T2E 8K5

Canada Toll-Free Credit Card Line (800) 665-5851
Canada Customer Service (403) 571-6363

On the Broadcast:
To contact the *Bible Answer Man* broadcast with
your questions, call toll free in the U.S. and Canada,
(888) ASK HANK (275-4265), Monday–Friday,
5:50 p.m. to 7:00 p.m. Eastern Time.

For a list of stations airing the *Bible Answer Man* broadcast,
or to listen online, log on to www.equip.org.

The Christian Research Institute (CRI) exists to provide Christians worldwide with carefully researched information and well-reasoned answers that encourage them in their faith and equip them to intelligently represent it to people influenced by ideas and teachings that assault or undermine orthodox, biblical Christianity. In carrying out this mission, CRI's strategy is expressed by the acronym *E-Q-U-I-P*:

The "E" in EQUIP represents the word *essentials*. CRI is committed to the maxim: "In essentials unity, in nonessentials liberty, and in all things charity."

The "Q" in the acronym EQUIP represents the word *questions*. In addition to focusing on essentials, CRI answers people's questions regarding cults, culture, and Christianity.

The "U" in the word EQUIP represents the word *user-friendly*. As much as possible, CRI is committed to taking complex issues and making them understandable and accessible to the lay Christian.

This brings us to the "I" in EQUIP, which stands for *integrity*. Recall Paul's admonition: "Watch your life and doctrine closely. Persevere in them, because if you do, you will save both yourself and your hearers."

Finally, the "P" in the acronym EQUIP represents the word *para-church*. CRI is deeply committed to the local church as the God-ordained vehicle for equipping, evangelism, and education.